BRICK WALL
WOOD SASH
CROWN GLASS
GLAZING BAR

TYPICAL GEORGIAN CORNICES.

PLAN.

QUOIN

PLINTH

STONE DRESSING

THE PERIOD HOUSE

STYLE, DETAIL & DECORATION
1774 – 1914

RICHARD RUSSELL LAWRENCE
& TERESA CHRIS

THE PERIOD HOUSE

STYLE, DETAIL & DECORATION
1774 – 1914

RICHARD RUSSELL LAWRENCE & TERESA CHRIS

WEIDENFELD & NICOLSON
LONDON

CONTENTS

THE PERIOD HOUSE: STYLE, DETAIL & DECORATION

1. INTRODUCTION

The Importance of Style 9

Classical and Palladian style 10

The Golden Age of
Georgian Architecture 12

The Terrace 13

The Building Act of 1774 15

2. LATE GEORGIAN 1774–1810

INTRODUCTION 17

LARGE —
front 20
plan 22
back 24

MEDIUM —
front 26
plan 28
back 30

SMALL —
front 32
plan 34
back 36

EPILOGUE 38

3. REGENCY & EARLY VICTORIAN 1811–50

INTRODUCTION 39

LARGE —
front 42
plan 44
back 46

MEDIUM —
front 48
plan 50
back 52

SMALL —
front 54
plan 56
back 58

EPILOGUE 60

7. DETAILS

Chimneys 128
Fireplaces 130
Cooking 132
Bathing 136
WCs and Privies 138
Lighting 140
Windows 142
Doors 144
Brick & Stone 146
Colour charts
  Georgian 148
  Regency &
    Early Victorian 149
  Mid-Victorian 150
  Late Victorian 151
  Edwardian 152
Paint effects 153
  Patterns 154
  Tiles 162
Information charts
  Population growth 164
  Urban Expansion 165
  Inventions & Technical
    Developments 166
  Historical
    Developments 167

Large, medium and small houses are each presented as front elevations, plans, cross-sections and backs.

front

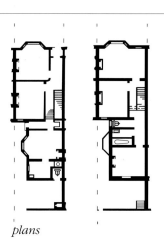

plans

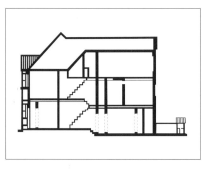

cross-section

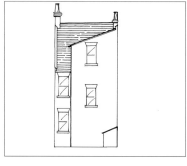

back

4. MID-VICTORIAN
1851–75

INTRODUCTION	61
LARGE –	
front	64
plan	66
back	68
MEDIUM –	
front	70
plan	72
back	74
SMALL –	
front	76
plan	78
back	80
EPILOGUE	82

5. LATE VICTORIAN
1876–99

INTRODUCTION	83
LARGE –	
front	86
plan	88
back	90
MEDIUM –	
front	92
plan	94
back	96
SMALL –	
front	98
plan	100
back	102
EPILOGUE	104

6. EDWARDIAN
1900–14

INTRODUCTION	105
LARGE –	
front	108
plan	110
back	112
MEDIUM –	
front	114
plan	116
back	118
SMALL –	
front	120
plan	122
back	124
EPILOGUE	126

Details – Bathing: p. 130–1

7. DETAILS (CONTINUED)

Ironwork	168
Roofs	170
Stairs	172
Mouldings	174
Walls	176

8. FURTHER INFORMATION

ILLUSTRATED GLOSSARY A-Z of terms used in this book	178
FURTHER INFORMATION Societies, museums, suppliers of authentic materials etc	187
BIBLIOGRAPHY	189

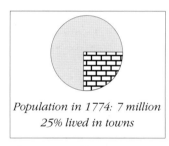

Population in 1774: 7 million 25% lived in towns

Charts: see p. 164–7

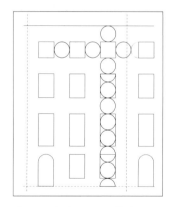

Illustrated Glossary: Palladian Proportions, see p. 172–80

A late Victorian ,medium sized terrace house

INTRODUCTION

People have an abiding interest in houses, particularly the houses they live in. Recent figures have shown that one-third of the population live in homes that were built before the First World War. A surprising percentage of the mortgages being taken out today are still on these older properties.

From the late Georgian period (1774) to the beginning of the First World War (1914) the proportion of the population living in towns and cities changed from a minority of twenty-five per cent to a majority of nearly eighty per cent. The population itself grew over four times, from seven and a half million to thirty-six million; in response, over six million urban houses were built. Those that remain still form one-third of the nation's housing stock. This book is intended for the occupants of or anyone interested in these older homes.

From its starting point in the late eighteenth century to the beginning of the First World War, the book is sub-divided into five different periods: Georgian, Regency & Early Victorian, Mid-Victorian, Late Victorian and Edwardian. Each period was characterised by its own distinct style. These styles not only followed each other chronologically but also overlapped and one style frequently borrowed features from another. The timing and pattern of the style changes are illustrated in the style chart on page three. This book is divided into five sections to cover each of the five styles.

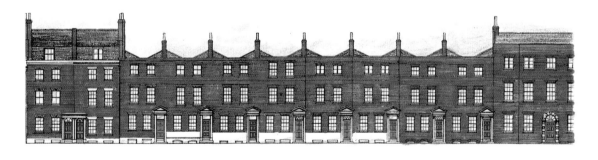

Late eighteenth-century Georgian terraced houses.

The three social classes familiar to us today, upper, middle and working, emerged as the population changed from a rural to a predominantly urban one. Each style section covers the equivalent houses for the three classes – large (upper), medium (middle) and small (working). The examples chosen in each section display the most easily identifiable features of the style for that size house. Those fortunate enough to live in older homes today will be able to find a typical example of a house similar to their own.

The sections show not only what the houses originally looked like but also how and why they were built and the way the first occupants used them. Each size of house is presented by a front, plan and back with both architectural and anecdotal information for each.

The major aspects of house design and decoration are dealt with individually in special spreads, and all the technical terms used throughout the book are illustrated in the glossary.

How the first occupants used them: a mid-nineteenth century kitchen.

THE IMPORTANCE OF STYLE

The style of both building and decor was important. Potential landlords and occupants wished to be up to date, although only those who did not fear criticism dared to be avant-garde. Style was dictated from the top of society downwards. Emulation was the order of the day.

Developers and builders were sensitive to fashion because houses were built speculatively. Ruin might face those left behind by the tide of change. The occupants themselves could move on when their leases expired, not so the luckless landlord. This was especially true at the upper end of the market.

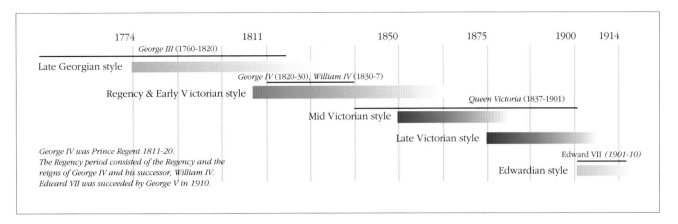

1774	1811	1850	1875	1900	1914

George III (1760-1820)

Late Georgian style

George IV (1820-30), William IV (1830-7)

Regency & Early Victorian style

Queen Victoria (1837-1901)

Mid Victorian style

Late Victorian style

Edward VII (1901-10)

Edwardian style

George IV was Prince Regent 1811-20.
The Regency period consisted of the Regency and the
reigns of George IV and his successor, William IV.
Edward VII was succeeded by George V in 1910.

OVERLAPPING STYLES

Usually, a new style appeared at the top end of the market while the older style continued lower down, so the styles overlapped.

As one might expect, the top end of the market was also the first to benefit from the latest technical developments. Often individual features of the new style were tacked on to the existing, creating transitional forms.

There were both regional and social variations of taste. For example, the Regency style remained popular in northern resort towns over half a century after its triumph in the capital.

ECLECTIC STYLES

From around 1850 onwards styles became more eclectic in form, taking inspiration from numerous sources. The predominant style also took several different forms. Each form shared distinctive features in both elevation and plan.

ATTITUDES TO STYLE

Attitudes to style were markedly different to our own. Prevalent opinion not only held that one style was correct but that others were morally inferior. This continued up to the end of the nineteenth century. At that time different criteria were applied to the question of style. For those who could afford it, style became an expression of their social opinions as well as their taste.

The lower down the social scale people found themselves, the less confidence they had in their own taste. This was particularly true of the middle classes, who were obsessed with appearing better than they were and wary of making a social faux pas by expressing their individual preference.

CLASSICAL AND PALLADIAN STYLE

Inigo Jones (d. 1652) lived before the Georgian period but he was responsible for establishing the 'classical' style of architecture in Britain. He had studied in Italy for several years and absorbed the Roman architecture and that of the Renaissance architect Andrea Palladio. On his return to England, he proceeded to design buildings in 'the good Roman manner' following the strict set of rules for classical proportions

Inigo Jones

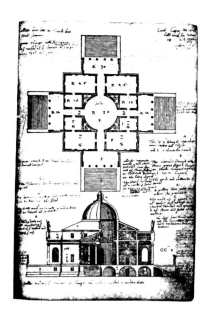

A page from Palladio, annotated by Jones during a visit to Italy.

drawn up by Palladio. The most famous of these were the Queen's House at Greenwich, the Whitehall Banqueting House and Covent Garden.

Inigo Jones worked as Surveyor to the Crown and executed his buildings under Court patronage. His designs were adopted by certain men of taste who became known as the Palladians.drawn up by Palladio. The most famous of these were the The re-assertion of strict Palladianism in the early eighteenth century was led by men such as Lord Burlington and the architect Colen Campbell. The uniformity of the Palladian style was compatible with the building of houses in congested towns suffering badly from overcrowding yet still expanding. It could also be executed in brick or stone. This made it an easy choice for conforming with the basic precautions against the spread of fire which

Above: The Whitehall Banqueting House.

Above: The first classically derived, speculatively built, terraced houses, designed by Inigo Jones as early as the 1630s. Top right: A view from the colonnades into the square. Above centre: Elevation of the Piazza, Covent Garden, showing St Paul's Church (centre) and the terraces (end on).

had come into force in London in the aftermath of the Great Fire (1666). These precautions against fire culminated in the 1774 London Building Act.

In Bath, the palatial uniformity of the terraces designed and built by John Wood the elder and John Wood the younger were vastly admired. The acceptability of the style grew further as the classical architecture of Italy became more familiar to members of the aristocracy. This was due to the popularity of the Grand Tour – a cultural progress through the most notable towns and sites of Europe which was regarded as the finishing school of the aristocracy. The components of the Palladian style could be copied by the 'spec' builders and adapted according to the size of plot available.

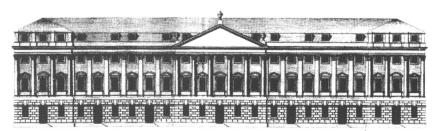

A Bath terrace designed and built by the Woods, father and son.

By 1774 Palladian designs had been widely disseminated by means of pattern books which were available not only to the Court and great patrons but right down through the classes to the humble carpenter and bricklayer. Palladianism was seen as the epitome of elegance and refinement. It was very un-English. The new buildings were in stark contrast to the timber-framed houses and buildings with gables, mullioned windows and wooden decoration in the form of brackets and carved barge-boards that had previously been the norm. Classical architecture in Britain has returned over and over again to Palladianism.

Above left: Timber-framed 'jetty' houses, before the changes of the seventeenth and eighteenth centuries.
Above right: A more rural form of the traditional gabled, timber-framed house.

The thirty years between the Peace of Paris and the beginning of the French wars has been described as the Golden Age of Georgian architecture. Success in war and the presence of a young spirited monarch on the English throne ushered in a new era, characterised by confidence and vitality, security and adventure, solid intellectual achievement and imaginative creation.

In architecture, William Chambers and Robert Adam were the pre-eminent personalities. Both men were from a similar background but their approach to design was radically different. Chambers was the complete academician, taking a leading role in the foundation of the Royal Academy; everything he designed was 'correct' and in good taste but often rather cold looking. His most important commissions were Somerset house on the Thames and Albany on Pall Mall.

Design by Sir William Chambers.

Adam, however, was impatient with the set forms of English tradition and aspired to be an innovator. Without rejecting classical forms, he began to use ornament – freely drawing upon Roman domestic decoration – and his influence slowly percolated down through the building trade. He had many imitators but his own major work – the Adelphi – has been largely destroyed. However, many of his private houses survive, for example, Chandos House, Chandos Street, 23 Grosvenor Square and 20 Portman Square. No love was

Interior design by Sir William Chambers.

Left: Part of a design by Robert Adam for a music room. Right: Fireplace design by Adam.

lost between Adam and Chambers (who called Adam's possessive, decorative innovations 'affectations'). Adam would have noththing to do with Chambers, nor was he ever a member of the Royal Academy.

THE TERRACE

The rich could enjoy their leisure in town: riding in the park.

During the Georgian period urban life became richer and more elaborate. The aristocracy was involved in public life more than ever and needed to be in the cities, especially London. Many of them actively sought to improve their fortunes by developing their urban land. Sizeable quality houses for wealthy occupants were an excellent venture, not only for those with landed income who were spending more time in town like London and Bath, but also for the professional classes, a group we take for granted today but who were then only evolving. Anyone who was anyone needed to be in town, especially for the Season.

SUCCESS OF THE TERRACE

London and other prominent towns embarked on an era of building during the Georgian period. This was a necessary step as towns had become overcrowded and were expanding at a brisk rate. The problem was not only how to house the many but also how to do it in a way that would satisfy the demands of taste, with well-proportioned, symmetrical building. The terrace was already an established solution. The basic plan of the terraced house had developed in the late seventeenth century; by the late eighteenth century it had become the dominant urban form. The street, rather than the house, was the basic architectural unit.

Left: The house in its own grounds – exceptional in towns. Right: What was there before the new terraces.

The face of towns was changed as the terrace, in the form of straight streets, crescents or squares, became the most common form of housing for all classes. Even the nobility, with a few exceptions, were content with a terraced house.

At the other end of the spectrum from the terrace was the 'villa', a detached house which stood in its own grounds. Apart from the exceptional houses of the very rich, the villa had become a rural rather than a typical urban dwelling.

A graciously designed estate with its church in the principal square.

If the villa stood in its own grounds, the new urban housing of the late eighteenth century had its own equivalent arrangements. These embraced not only the home but the whole environment around it: a town had to have its park. To achieve this ideal in the new urban housing, each terrace had to have its square and the street its trees. When these ideas were well executed, the developments also included markets, churches and smaller housing to accommodate those providing services.

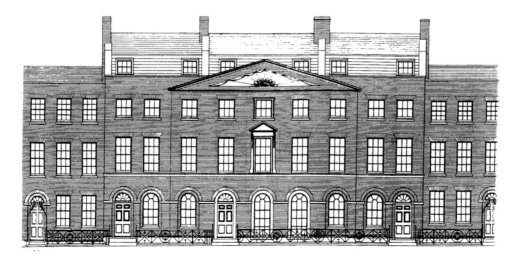

Palatial uniformity was achieved by emphasising the centre and end blocks of the terrace.

PALATIAL UNIFORMITY

The rich were happy to move into these new 'terraced' houses because they looked so grand. It appeared as if they were living in a palace, even though they actually occupied only a slice of it. At the top end of the market, terraces differed from the others by emphasising the centre and ends with large scale classical features, turning them into imposing blocks. Gigantic columns and pediments and other decorative additions introduced symmetry and palatial uniformity.

HIERARCHY

Vertical hierarchy.

Terraces had their own hierarchy. The centre was the most desirable, followed by the end blocks. The individual terraced house also had a distinct hierarchy. This worked vertically rather than horizontally. From the outside the first floor was given the most emphasis, then the ground and second floors. The first floor was also given the largest windows and the most decorative detail. The remaining upper storeys were more modest. The servants' quarters – the basement and the attic – were half-hidden, at the bottom by area railings and at the top by a parapet.

THE LONDON BUILDING ACT OF 1774

After the Great Fire of London many building acts and statutes were passed to try and prevent such disasters from happening again. The London Building Act of 1774 was a landmark of its kind. Intended to reduce the risk of fire spreading, it specified structural dimensions for new houses which it divided into four 'rates' according to their value and size.

These are the 'rates' that applied to terraced houses and provided the new classifications, which included descriptions of the occupants themselves:

Rate	Occupants	Value	Size
FIRST	Nobility	Over £850	Over 900 sq ft *(Great or exceptional)*
SECOND	Merchants	£300–£850	500–900 sq ft *(Large)*
THIRD	Clerks	£150–£300	350–500 sq ft *(Medium)*
FOURTH	Mechanics	Up to £150	Up to 350 sq ft *(Small)*

Old streets built before the building acts.

The London Building Act of 1774 spelled out the structural code for foundations, thickness of external and internal walls and the position of windows for each 'rate' of house. These standards were meant to become the minimum requirements for London boroughs. This contributed to greater uniformity than ever before and only the largest houses were not so rigidly designed.

The second, third and fourth rates of houses became very stereotyped, especially as the Act also forbade any form of extraneous woodwork. In many ways this was an excellent development. It gave a degree of order and dignity to the new estates being built and established a standard of housing for the urban working class, which would have provided them with decent accommodation if there had been any legislation against overcrowding.

The Act only applied to metropolitan areas but it represented 'good practice' everywhere. It influenced other local building regulations, creating whole streets of the same social class for the first time.

FULL CIRCLE

In the late Georgian period houses being built in towns became highly standardised across the entire social range. In the following century the design of housing went through various incarnations but by the First World War it had come full circle and Neo-Georgian homes were being built once again as the style of choice and economy.

Full circle: Eighteenth-century Georgian style (left) and early twentieth-century Edwardian (right).

LATE GEORGIAN
1774-1810

The entire Georgian period stretched from 1714 to 1837 and included the Regency era (1811–1837). This section covers the years 1774–1810 (up to the beginning of the Regency). During this time classical proportions were not only applied to large houses but to the whole social range – large, medium and small.

George III was on the throne. From mid-century the population had begun to grow and also to change from being predominantly rural to predominantly urban. Commerce and industry fluctuated, but overall the result was greater

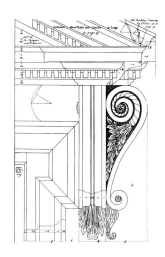

wealth for large sections of society. Technological innovations affected the means of production, the most radical of them being the steam engine. The colonies provided export markets for the textiles and manufactured goods which were now being produced in such large numbers.

Greater prosperity enabled more people from the top end of society to make the Grand Tour and be exposed to other cultures, particularly the classical. They were extremely impressed by what they saw and their views filtered down – many became infected with an enthusiasm for everything classical which, in turn, became synonymous with the notion of 'good taste'. Classical learning had

Above left: Classical forms inspired enthusiasm – detail from a mid-century pattern book.

Well laid out, classically inspired buildings: an eighteenth-century square in Bath.

long commanded respect, Latin being the language of the educated. Influential people also felt a political affinity with ancient Rome. and it was only natural that those who looked up to them adopted their cultural preference.

Georgian houses appeared in a complete range of sizes – the small one was the latest to appear in the final quarter of the eighteenth century. By then it was one style in a variety of different sizes, thus catering for upper, middle and lower classes. In towns such as London and Bath, which were both leisure and political centres, there was a significant proportion of large houses. In commercial centres a significant proportion of the housing stock was made up of medium houses, and in industrial centres the majority of new houses built were small.

STANDARDISATION

Many of the building components were produced locally, with notable exceptions such as Welsh slate and Baltic timber. However, building practice had become standardised to such an extent that the components, such as windows

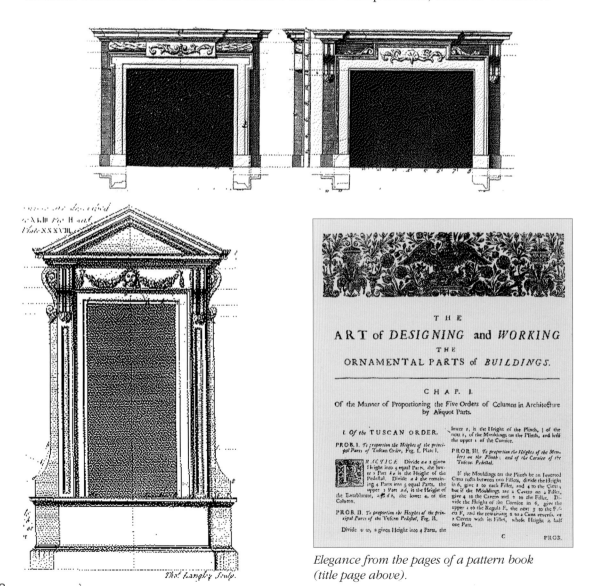

Elegance from the pages of a pattern book (title page above).

and even the bricks themselves, were becoming similar in size. There were two main reasons for this, Building Acts and pattern books.

BUILDING ACTS AND PATTERN BOOKS

There had been numerous building acts since the Great Fire of London in 1666. Other cities had had their fires too. The 1774 London Building Act was both stringent and effective. Its strictures were not only enforced in London but adopted throughout the country as 'good practice'.

These strictures were primarily concerned with preventing the spread of fire but led to the standardisation of building design. This standardisation was made possible by numerous, easily obtainable and well-produced pattern books. The pattern books covered everything from delicate details to entire terraces.

They were produced by printers and publishers and cost a few shillings each – one or two days' wages for a craftsman in the building trades. The developer only needed to give the briefest specification to the builder. All that was necessary was a sketch and a few measurements which were sometimes scribbled on the back of legal documents; his *Builder's Companion*, *Builder's Jewel* or *Workman's Director* could provide the rest. Proportions, dimensions, structure and decoration were all comprehensively illustrated and explained. The work of the better known authors such as Langley, Pain and later Nicholson and Loudon was referred to by contemporary commentators, speculators, builders and craftsmen alike. Well-thumbed copies, their cover boards removed, were carried on site in the builders' back pockets.

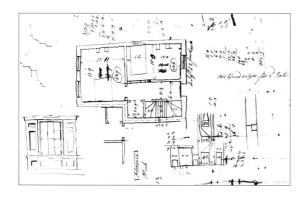

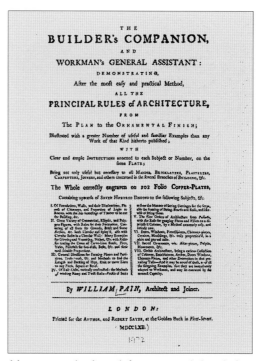

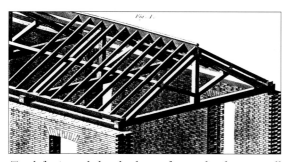

Top left: Actual sketch plans of a modest house – all a builder required. Above left: Structural details from Nicholson. Right: Title page of Pain's Builder's Companion.

LARGE – *front*

WHAT WAS GEORGIAN STYLE?

Late Georgian style was highly standardised. The key features of the design were proportion, order and symmetry.

Houses were flat fronted, and had plain brick or stone facades with cambered arches over the windows. The most important rooms were given the largest windows. The colour of the brick depended on the locality but the most common colour was a rusty brown.

CHARACTERISTIC FEATURES

The most characteristic features were a semi-circular fan light above the front door, a simple string course at first-floor level and an unadorned parapet which guarded the eaves. Under the 1774 London Building Act exposed timber was banned as a fire hazard.

A few steps led up to the front door. Many houses had 'areas' in front of the basement to provide that lowest floor with light. Wrought iron railings surrounded the area at street level. Steps from the street down to the area had only just become common.

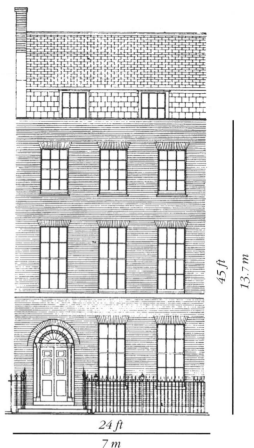

A large house with two-leaf front door. The door perfectly aligned with the window above it. The house would have been classified as Second Rate under the 1774 London Building Act.

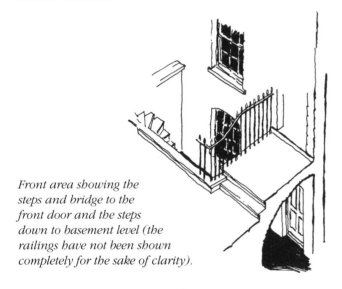

Front area showing the steps and bridge to the front door and the steps down to basement level (the railings have not been shown completely for the sake of clarity).

A very large front area, showing the steps, railings and drain. Coal came in at the front through a hole in the pavement and was stored in the cellar immediately underneath (doorway seen on the right). Ash from the fires was stored in the next cellar. A large house produced approximately eleven tonnes of ash annually. The ash was collected three times a year.

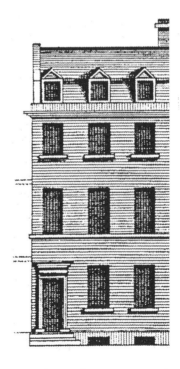

A design drawn up in 1747.

A large house built in stone.

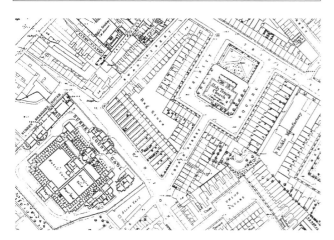

An estate plan shows streets, squares and mews.

Shrubbery walls and grass plots in the squares afforded
seasonable relief.

WHO LIVED THERE?
The people who lived in the
large houses ranged from
the nobility and land-
owning class down to
prosperous merchants. They
did not own the houses –
although they received
substantial incomes from
their own properties and
businesses – and they were
content to pay rent.

COSTS
Before the wars of the late eighteenth century this rent
could be calculated as one fourteenth of the cost of
building the house. The basic cost of houses of this type
was £550–£650, so the rent might be £40–£50 a year and
was probably paid quarterly.

WHO OWNED THEM?
The purpose of building houses was to create income
from the rents. The person to whom the rent was paid,
the 'landlord', didn't necessarily own the ground on
which the house stood. However, the landlord definitely
owned the lease.

The owner of the ground would have it 'improved' which
meant laying out roads and services. Once this was done
an improved ground rent could be charged.

Sometimes the ground landlord and house landlord were
the same, as in the larger estates which were often
responsible for the building of this class of house. These
were usually the best managed and cared for and
consequently the most sought after.

BUILDING LEASES
Building leases were a system of speculation by the
hereditary landlords which brought much of the new
urban areas into being. The landlord would divide his
property into plots which were let at a low ground rent
on the understanding that the lessee built, at his own
expense, a house or number of houses of substantial
character. These houses, at the end of the lease, became
the property of the ground landlord.

The great estates could not be sold except by an Act of
Parliament. By the lease system the land, with very little
modification, could be made profitable while still under
the original ownership. The system has remained to this
day. The original leases were for as little as 33 years but
by the end of the Georgian period leases of 99 years
were common.

LARGE – *plan*

BASIC PATTERN

The basic pattern of the large Georgian house was two rooms on each floor, arranged one behind the other.

During this period every room developed a specific function – something which was unknown before. For example, until then a collapsible table had been pulled out for use when dining. But at this end of the market, houses now began to be designed with a permanent dining room and installed with dining furniture.

PIANO NOBILE

The first floor was the focal floor of the house and was called, in the Italian manner, the 'piano nobile'. It contained the main reception rooms where the most important guests would be received. It also enjoyed the 'prospect', the pleasing view. Lesser beings were shown into the morning room or study on the ground floor.

UPSTAIRS, DOWNSTAIRS

Bedrooms were on the second and third floors. The servants slept in the attic rooms, often two or three to a bed.

The kitchen was in the basement which was entirely the province of the servants.

DEVELOPMENTS

There was a small extension to the main body of the house at the back on the ground floor. This contained a 'closet' or 'retiring room'.

Fireplaces were now situated centrally in the party walls.

Panelling began to be replaced by plaster.

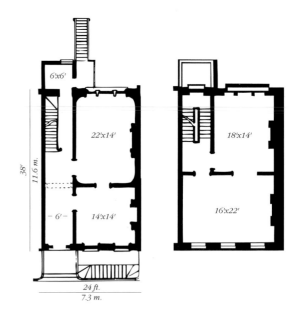

Above: Ground and first-floor plans with a small rear extension. Such an extension was often referred to as the closet wing.

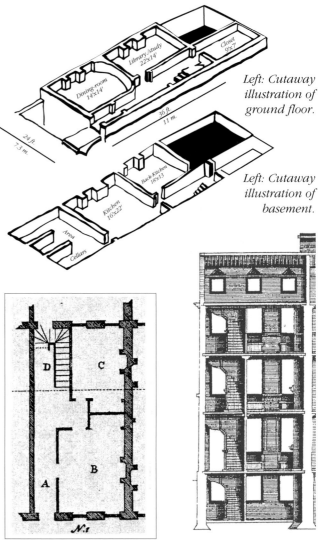

Left: Cutaway illustration of ground floor.

Left: Cutaway illustration of basement.

Above left: A ground-floor plan of the type which was to become standard, drawn in 1747. Above right: Section through the house in the 1747 plan (elevation on page 20).

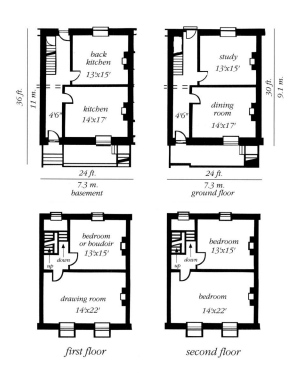

Standard plans for basement, ground, first and second floors of a Second Rate house without a rear extension under the 1774 London Building Act.

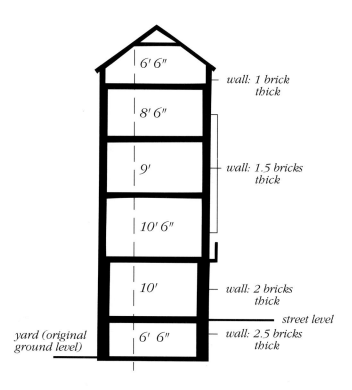

Cross-section showing variations in room heights and thickness of walls on different floors.

THE ARCHITECT

The rise of individual architects was one of the greatest influences on the new manner of building in the Georgian period. Until then houses and other buildings had been planned by people acting on behalf of, or from within such bodies as the Church or the town council.

Client, architect (centre) and craftsman.

Until about halfway through the eighteenth century there was no such thing as a profession of architects as we know it today. Anyone who designed a building could call themselves an architect. They were tradesmen, surveyors and the gentry.

Some gentlemen with a passion for building, notably Vanbrugh and Burlington, took it up. Other distinguished architects were often craftsmen by training. After about 1763, however, architecture became a recognisable profession and the men who belonged to it were more than just anyone with a 'rule of thumb' capacity for design.

In 1791 a group of London architects formed a dining club, a typical example of the growing professionalism within society.

THE SURVEYOR

The surveyor's profession was an old one – it harked back to Tudor times. Unlike the so-called 'architects', the surveyor was educated and specifically trained for his profession. He was qualified not only to survey the land and measure it for estimating and pricing, but also to supervise the building work. Both Inigo Jones and Christopher Wren held the position of King's Surveyor.

THE MASTER-BUILDER

The houses themselves were built not by a building company, but by a group of independent craftsmen brought together by someone called a 'master-builder'. Often trained as a bricklayer or carpenter, his role became that of a businessman. He would not necessarily have a team of men working for him but would hire the appropriate craftsmen as needed. The master-builder was of great importance as it was he who initiated the construction of entire houses and built them for the speculative market.

The master-builder, although one of the pivotal figures in the building trade, was still inferior, socially if not financially, to the surveyor.

LARGE – *back*

THE BACK MEANT SERVICES

The back meant services. There the yard was an additional work space for the servants.

THE PRIVY AND THE SMOKE

The ground immediately to the rear of the house would be paved and the rest covered with gravel, which had to be regularly raked as it became blackened by soot from the house fires. The level of the yard was the original ground level.

The privy would be here, with the cesspit either underneath or close by. There would also be a rain-water butt.

The principle cause of dust and rubbish was the residue of coal fires: ash and cinders. The paving acts of 1762 had improved street cleanliness by forbidding the public to throw any kind of 'dust' into the street; they now had to keep it for collection by the 'dustmen'.

Ideally the back would have access for the nightsoil men and also accommodate a 'mews' building for horses, carriages and their attendants.

LOOKING DOWN ON THE BACK

The family looked down on the back because the ground floor at this end of the building was actually one floor up. They might never go there to use the privy, instead using a pot that would be emptied by a servant.

> The street front smelt of horse dung and the back of the house of human waste.

The rear of an eighteenth-century house situated at the end of a terrace in north London. Towards the end of the eighteenth century gardens like this became rarer as urban land became more and more valuable.

Line drawing of the scene illustrated above: The outhouse (1) accommodated the privy (usually nearest the house), coal, ash, lumber and tools. The paved terrace (2) made access to the privy easier, as well as housing potted plants.

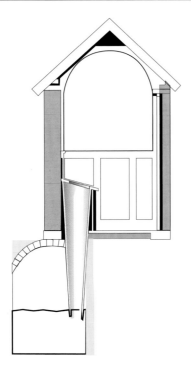

Cross-section of a privy: This design was built directly over the cesspool.

Cold Water	Kitchen Range	WC
limited supply	possibly early type	probably not

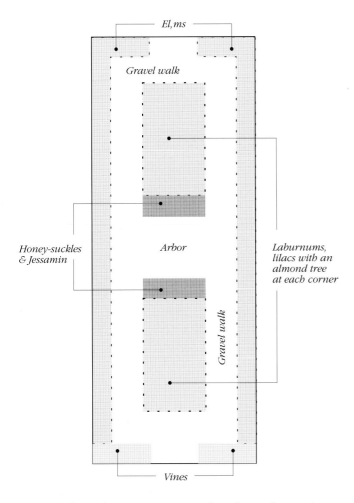

An eighteenth-century town garden plan with gravel walks, flower-beds and a central arbor. The gravel had to be turned regularly because it quickly went black from the soot in the air.

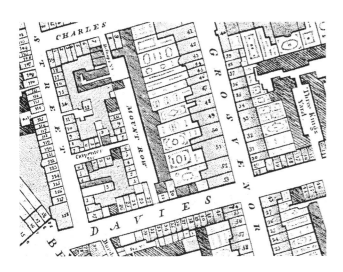

A map made in 1790 shows how many houses still had gardens and also nearby clusters of mews buildings (see REGENCY – Large back).

BOG-HOUSES

Spacious 'bog-houses' or privies were built at the end of the garden. Privies had numerous colloquial names such as 'jakes' or 'Jericho' houses.

In the larger house the privy was landscaped into the garden design and tastefully camouflaged. A brick-lined circular pit was constructed under it and connected to the main drain. Water was sometimes laid on to flush these receptacles.

Some of the larger houses had drains. They were constructed of brick and laid just under the floors of the cellar. Unfortunately, they were usually poorly constructed and leaks were commonplace, making the houses unsavoury and creating a health hazard.

These drains were connected to public sewers under the roads and the untreated sewage was channelled into the nearest river. If no public sewer was available, the waste went into the cesspool in the garden.

Cesspits were emptied at night by the nightsoil men.

EARLY WCs

Only the largest of the Georgian houses and a few of the medium sized were fitted with the first WCs. Alexander Cummings patented his WC in 1775 and Joseph Bramagh produced a more reliable model three years later.

The 'necessary' had only recently made its first appearance inside the house itself by means of the new closet extensions built for it.

THE NIGHTSOIL MAN

Nightsoil men, or 'nightmen', were bound by law to work only between midnight and dawn. The only disadvantage to this was that they provided another disturbance. They were paid for removing the waste and money could also be made by selling the raw sewage as fertiliser.

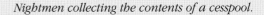

Nightmen collecting the contents of a cesspool.

MEDIUM – *front*

SIZE

The medium-sized house fell into Rate Three of the housing classification, so the average building cost was £150–£300.

Basically, the major difference between the medium and the large was that it was smaller. The height from ground to parapet varied from 29ft to 46ft. The width ranged from 16ft to 24ft.

CONTINUING PATTERN

Trying to follow the classical proportions of the larger houses, the medium had the same basic configuration of rooms but with fewer storeys.

It was not so finely fitted out in terms of external decoration. Usually, all it could show was a simple string course, window arches and modest wrought-iron work for the balconies.

LIGHT

They managed to fit two windows per floor with fanlights over the doors. Without the fanlight the hall would have had no natural light.

It was hard to achieve the proportions apparent on larger houses. However, the largest windows were still on the first floor and the windows on the storeys above aligned with them. Unfortunately, the medium-sized houses were not wide enough to allow the front door to be aligned directly under a first-floor window.

c.31 ft

c.19 ft

c.5.8 m

It was impossible to align the door and windows of the ground floor with those above it. Instead, the ground floor could be picked out by rendering it in plaster, thus dividing it from the parts of the facade with which it was out of alignment.

THE RENT

The rent would have been from £12 to £25 a year. The approximate building cost ranged from £150–£300.

A terrace of medium-sized houses.

Design for a medium-sized house drawn in 1790. The front door could be positioned to the side because the house was at the end of a terrace. The ground-floor front room benefited from the additional space available.

WHO LIVED THERE?

The medium-sized houses were classified as for 'Tradesmen', 'Opulent Tradesmen' and 'Merchants'. They might also accommodate professionals of modest means. This 'middle class' formed a growing proportion of the population in centres of commerce.

WHO BUILT THEM?

Streets of medium-sized houses tended to be built on smaller plots of land than the up-market large. The developers themselves were also of more modest means, as were the builders. A terrace could be constructed by several different builders, consequently there was likely to be some variation in the row or terrace.

The variations were not extreme because of the standardisation of design and materials.

Bricklayers

Carpenters

The kitchen of a medium-sized house was usually at the front as long as it was light enough.

Bricklayers, stonemasons and carpenters were the three senior craftsmen because they had the most work to do. They were usually the most educated of the trades and took the lead where building contracts were concerned.

Left: Brickmaking – bricks were made locally, near the building site, from local materials.

MEDIUM – *plan*

HIERARCHY WITHIN THE HOME

The medium-sized house struggled to maintain the piano nobile – and hence have three reception rooms – at the cost of more bedrooms. This was done not out of a sense of social ambition but out of a notion of propriety. In practice, the use of rooms was, of necessity, more flexible than in the large house. If there was no attic space, servants would have to sleep where they worked – in the kitchen.

DOG-LEG

To make the most use of the limited space available in the medium-sized house a style of staircase named the dog-leg was utilised. Following the example of the large houses, this was now positioned at the back.

FURTHER DEVELOPMENTS

Access to all main rooms was from the corridors. Upstairs there was a minimum of two to three bedrooms. If the house had an attic, the rooms would have square ceilings.

Houses in this range were usually 23ft–29ft deep and 16ft–20ft wide, with an overall area of not more than 500 square feet.

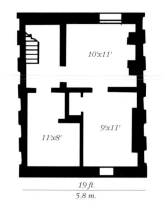

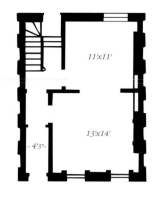

Basement: This example only has a lightwell, rather than an area, at the front. The adjacent room was probably used as a store because it is unlit by any type of window.

Ground floor

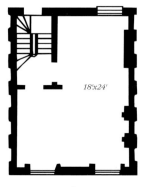

First floor

Second floor

Lighting – Left: Eighteenth-century depiction of a family group. Except on formal occasions, candles were simply carried from room to room. Right: Depiction of how dim an interior was when lit by oil lamps and candles.

FOUR LEVELS OF LIFE – *How they would run their day*

	Rising	Breakfast	Dinner	Work Ends	tea	Supper
Journeyman	5–6am	6–9am	12–1pm	6pm	5–6	hours later
Tradesman	8am	6–9am	1–4.30pm		5–6	9pm
Merchant		9,10 or 11am	4,5,6pm		hours later	9pm
Nobility		12–1pm	5,6,7pm			0–2am

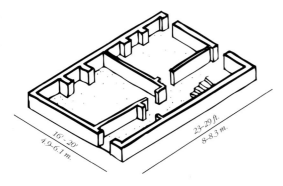

Perspective view of the ground floor.

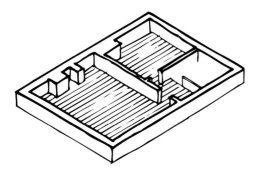

Perspective view of the first floor.

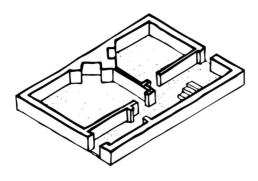

Perspective view of the ground floor. This arrangement of the fireplaces was fairly common earlier in the eighteenth century.

SUB-LETTING

Medium-sized houses were frequently occupied by more than one family. This was often the case if the original tenants could not afford the rent for the whole house themselves. They would sub-let rooms, often in pairs, or suites, on each floor. Landlords would try to ensure that this didn't happen because it lowered the tone and value of their property. Some estates actually prohibited sub-letting.

HIERARCHY OF CRAFTS

The Georgian building trade was made up of craftsmen, each trained in a particular skill. They were first apprenticed for seven years, then worked as journeymen. The good ones were men of considerable skill and well-respected in the community. The entrepreneurial ones often set up on their own.

Hierarchy of crafts:

Masons
Bricklayers
Carpenters
Joiners
Plasterers
Paviors
Plumbers
Glaziers
Locksmiths
Carvers
Painters

Plumbers were responsible for lead roofing and guttering.

There was a definite hierarchy among the crafts. The stonemason, the bricklayer and the carpenter came out on top. They could generally read and 'make out a draft' of a 'dwelling-house', probably drawing on the many pattern books available.

It was either the bricklayer or the mason, depending on whether the local building material was brick or stone, closely followed by the carpenter, who was responsible for the structural woodwork: floors, ceiling, roof etc. These three had most of the work on the house, hence their pre-eminence. One of them was usually the 'master-builder'.

DAY AND PAY

Journeymen were paid 2s 6d a day by the master craftsmen when they needed additional competent help.

They all worked a ten-hour day, starting at 6am.

Labourers did the coarse work like excavation and carrying materials. They received 1s 8d a day.

BUILDERS' BARTER

These craftsmen often worked on each other's contracts and consequently a system of barter was widespread. Houses were frequently built with very little money actually changing hands.

The individual craftsmen obtained their own materials more or less directly from the source; bricks from the local brickyard, timber from the sawyer.

LATE GEORGIAN 1774-1810

MEDIUM – *back*

FOLLOW THE MODEL

The back was similar to that of the larger size house: the ground level was that of the basement, which connected to a small yard. This yard was confined to services.

The medium was less likely to have cellars at the front under the pavement, in which case all the essential services – coal, ash, water and cess – would have been located at the rear.

The piped water supply was very limited and it was unlikely that this size of house would have had water on tap. Rainwater, collected in a butt at back, would have been useful and they would have obtained the rest of their water from the public source or an itinerant water carrier.

The privy or bog house would be located as far away from the house as possible, but often that wasn't very far and odious fumes were prevalent.

This size house usually lacked direct access to the rear, therefore the nightsoil men would have to go through the house itself to empty the cesspit. Coalmen and dustmen would also have to use the front entrance.

Backyards as small as 10ft deep accommodated a privy, coal bin, drain and a water butt. Everything had to be carried through the house.

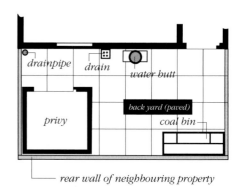

Plan of the yard shown above.

Dust Oy–Eh! was the cry of the dust collector.

Nightmen filling their cart with the contents of the privy or cesspool. Even the nightmen had to use the front door when there was no other access.

Cold Water	Kitchen Range	WC
limited supply	possibly early type	No

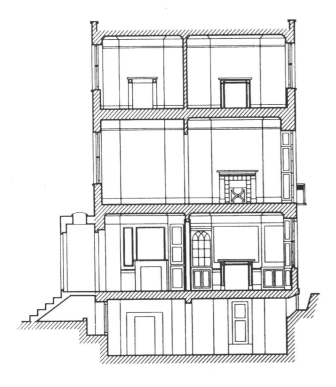

Cross-section of a house which only has a lightwell (not an area) at the front (right) and steps down to the rear at the back.

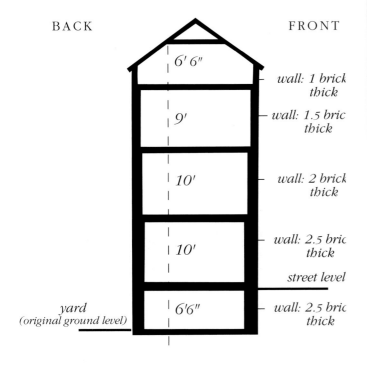

BACK   FRONT

6' 6"   *wall: 1 brick thick*

9'   *wall: 1.5 bric thick*

10'   *wall: 2 brick thick*

10'   *wall: 2.5 bric thick*

     street level

yard (original ground level)   6'6"   *wall: 2.5 bric thick*

Cross-section showing variations in room heights and thickness of walls on different floors.

COAL

If the medium did not have cellars under the pavement at the front, coal had to be carried through the house itself and stored at the back.

Ash from the fires was similarly stored and collected about three times a year. Residue from the coal fires was the principal cause of dust and rubbish, though the amount of ash produced by the mediums was less than the eleven tonnes produced by the large houses.

RECYCLING

The parish was responsible for collection and it was put out to private tender. Companies paid for the privilege of collecting the 'dust'. It was a valuable commodity and recycled at the dust heaps, where it was sieved and separated.

Fine dust, known as 'soil', was used as preparation for reclaimed marshland. The lumps, referred to as 'brieze', were sold to the brickyards to make cheap 'place' bricks.

DUST OY–EH!

The dustmen announced their presence by crying 'Dust oy-eh!' They were often employed by the same contractors as the street-cleaners, who were known as 'scavengers'. Scavengers shovelled mud and horse-muck off the street. The latter was also recyclable.

RAG AND BOTTLE SHOPS

All other household rubbish could be disposed of into the second-hand trades. Itinerant street traders called, eager to snap up anything, particularly rags. Rags were worth up to 3d a pound. Good white linen was at the top of the list as it was used to make paper.

A rag-picker

SMALL – *front*

BASIC MINIMUM

The most obvious difference in design of the Georgian small house was the number of windows. The small houses often had only one on each floor, aligned one above the other.

The windows were sashes, but they might not have been 'hung', in which case they had to be wedged open with wooden chocks. The small Georgian house occasionally had external shutters for security and insulation.

These houses still had a fanlight and window arches which were either flat or segmental; otherwise there was no external decoration, just a flat brick wall.

VARIATIONS

Some might have a cockloft or dormer window, providing light for an attic room. Many houses were built with workrooms, or loomshops, on the top floor. These often had large windows to give better working light. Alternatively, workrooms were also found in the basement where the light was correspondingly bad.

In contrast to earlier industrial housing, an increasing proportion of these new houses had no provision for workspace and were purely dwellings. They were small but they did separate work from home life.

They were less than 29ft high from ground to parapet and usually less than 16ft wide. They would have been classed as Fourth rate under the 1774 London Building Act.

24 ft 6 in / 7.5 m

14 ft 6 in
4.4 m

A well-built small terraced house.

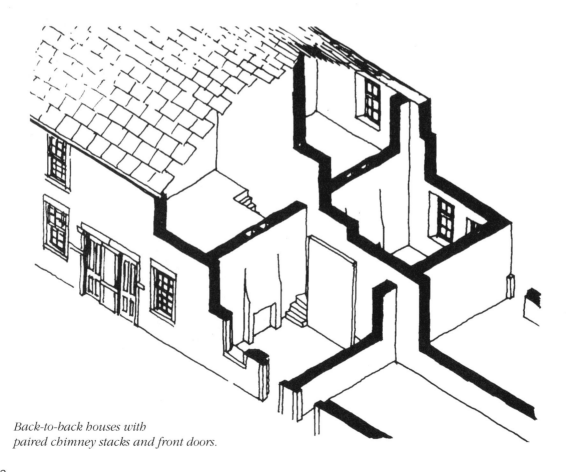

Back-to-back houses with paired chimney stacks and front doors.

A terrace of small houses. The pairing of the doors had a decorative effect and allowed the entrance to be situated on the opposite side of the living-room to the fireplace. Note the paired chimney stacks.

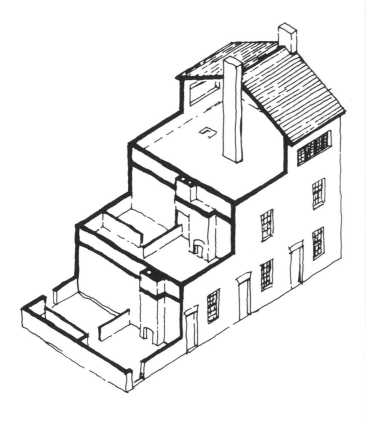

Through houses with a top-floor loomshop which was shared by the occupants of the houses. The large windows on that floor gave better light for working. Each front door entered on the opposite side of the room to the fireplace.

WHO LIVED THERE?

The skilled and semi-skilled workforce who moved into the newly built small urban houses were referred to as 'mechanics'. They needed to live close to the mill or factory because their long working hours left little time for travel to and fro.

There were also still numerous semi-independent textile workers, spinners, weavers and hosiers, who worked in loomshops above their homes. They also wanted to be close to the 'middlemen' – the entrepreneurs from whom they obtained their raw materials and to whom they sold the finished article.

During this period they were often among the most prosperous workers in the textile industry. Consequently, they were able to afford accommodation with work space in the new urban centres.

SHODDY BUILDING

Although the terraces of the smallest Georgian houses externally resembled those of the largest, the potential for only a low rent led to shoddy building.

It was a widely held opinion that this was the only way in which they could be built profitably. So widespread was this belief that many of the 'tricks of the trade' were condoned by even the best informed commentators. Common tricks of the trade were the use of snapped headers (bricks broken in half) instead of a full brick to bond the inner and outer skins of the wall; the substitution of poor-quality bricks; and timber, which rotted, being used to strengthen weak walls. So although the dimensions of the houses were predetermined, the materials and workmanship were often poor.

In order to realise any profit, builders skimped their work – a practice often forced upon them by the inflated price of land and materials due to the Napoleonic Wars which went on for over twenty years from 1793-1814. Building costs during this time almost doubled because materials were hard to come by as they were being used for military installations.

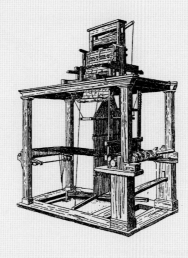

Left: A Jacquard-loom of the kind which might have been installed in the top floor 'loomshops'.

LATE GEORGIAN 1774-1810

SMALL – *plan*

TWO BASIC TYPES

The plan of the small Georgian house reveals two basic types – the through house and the back-to-back.

THROUGH HOUSES

The 'through house' was a very small house without hall, corridors or basement. Entrance from the street was directly into the living-room. The kitchen was behind the living-room.

The stairs to the first floor were 'winders', usually situated in a corner of the kitchen and rising directly into one of the two bedrooms.

BACK-TO-BACKS

The 'back-to-back' house was an ingenious invention which divided a through house into two laterally and often added a basement and an attic. As the back-to-back house was only one room deep, it enabled double the number of houses to be built on the same amount of land. It was also cheaper to build because it had three common, or 'party', walls.

The quality of construction of the original back-to-backs was good and they provided a standard of urban housing which compared favourably to that which their occupants might have obtained in the country.

They were well up on the housing scale and were soon to be found in large numbers in Manchester, Liverpool, Leeds, Bradford, Nottingham, the Potteries and Birmingham.

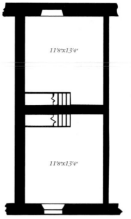

Pair of back-to-backs: first floor (note lack of fireplaces).

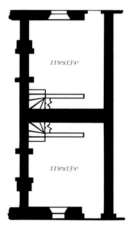

Pair of back-to-backs: ground floor (with fireplace).

Another back-to-back arrangement with entrance through the basement (See cross-section, left-hand house).

Back-to-back: first floor.

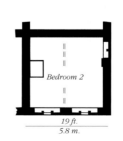

Back-to-back: Second floor.

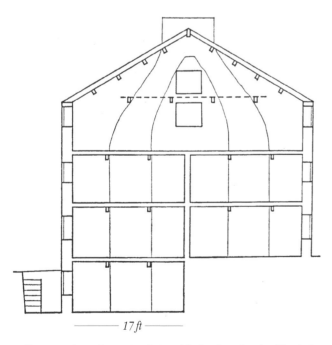

Cross-section of a pair of sizeable back-to-backs: The left-hand house had a cellar through which the house was entered. The top floor accommodated a shared loomshop. Access to the loomshop was through the right-hand house.

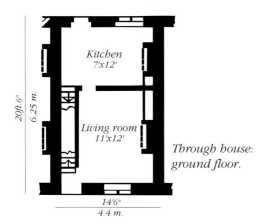

Through house: ground floor.

20ft.6"
6.25 m.

Kitchen
7'x12'

Living room
11'x12'

14'6"
4.4 m.

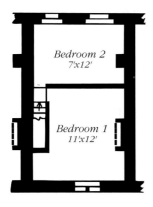

Bedroom 2
7'x12'

Bedroom 1
11'x12'

Through house: first floor.

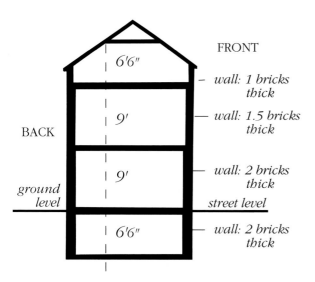

FRONT

6'6"

wall: 1 bricks thick

9'

wall: 1.5 bricks thick

BACK

9'

wall: 2 bricks thick

ground level

street level

6'6"

wall: 2 bricks thick

Cross-section showing variations in room heights and thickness of walls on different floors.

WHY BACK-TO-BACKS?

The early back-to-backs were built on small, individually owned plots of land. Many of the plots of land in the new industrial areas were long and thin. This was the result of enclosure, when commonly held land had been divided up into individually owned strips. These small 'parcels' of land were often the only ones available for building small houses. They were often built on spaces which had previously been yards and gardens.

DOUBLE YOUR MONEY

Local building regulations usually specified a minimum street width of about thirty feet, so building through houses along a properly constituted street was scarcely a profitable plan to adopt.

Two back-to-backs and a street could be built on the same amount of land as a single through house and a street. The rent for two back-to-backs was one third more than that of a single through house.

The back-to-back design could also be built singly, rather than as a pair, to use up any available land – perhaps in the hope of the neighbouring plot becoming available so that the pair could be completed.

COURTS

Court developments, which shared a communal yard and services, made even greater use of the available land.

Another characteristic of court development was the end wall, against which the privies were often built. This actually marked the boundary of that particular property or 'Rents', as areas of small housing were sometimes known.

OCCUPANCY

In areas which adopted the back-to-back, the number of through houses was a small proportion of the total. Elsewhere, it was common for different families to share a through house if they couldn't get one by themselves. Multiple occupation of this sort obviously made it difficult to keep the dwelling salubrious. So the through houses had their problems too.

A communal water pump, referred to as 'the tree in the street'. It was made of elm wood as were the pipes.

SMALL – *back*

THERE WERE NO BACKS

It seems like stating the obvious, but the back-to-backs did not have backs. They either faced the street or inward onto a communal yard or 'court' with one open side.

COURTS

Back-to-backs were often built around three sides of a square. This created a central yard, the court. The court contained all the communal or shared services – the privy/privies and ash bins.

Houses facing on to the street were more prestigious and commanded a higher rent.

THROUGHS

The most highly skilled workers got the through houses. In some areas these even had front gardens and allotments.

The privy was in the tiny back yard, alternatively they would have had to use a 'privy pail'.

Only the front door on these houses was made of hardwood. The back door and all the internal doors were made from the cheaper, newly available softwood planks.

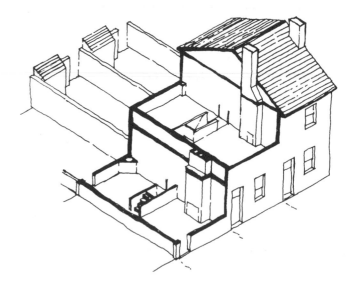

Through houses with their own yards. These examples had their own privies and access from a service lane at the back.

Cold Water	Kitchen Range	WC
No	No	No

Small houses for the workers were built wherever the need arose. The oldest and largest industry – textiles – was located in the Midlands, hosiery in Leicester, Nottingham and the West Yorkshire towns, including Leeds, and cotton in Lancashire. Market towns grew as 'retail' centres of agriculture; other towns as centres for industries such as mining, metal/iron and other manufactured goods. As production increased, ports also expanded – Liverpool being the prime example.

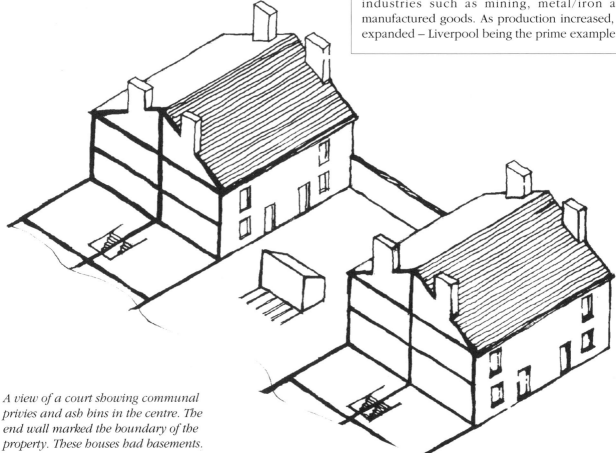

A view of a court showing communal privies and ash bins in the centre. The end wall marked the boundary of the property. These houses had basements.

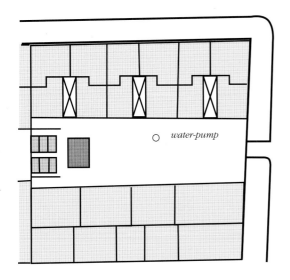

A court which had the open side facing the street. This was the best arrangement because it allowed easy access for the removal of ash, rubbish and cess. This court also had its own water pump.

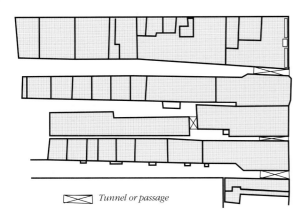

⊠ *Tunnel or passage*

Often the only land available for the building of small houses were thin strips of land left over from the medieval system of farming. The result was developments like these burgages in Leeds.

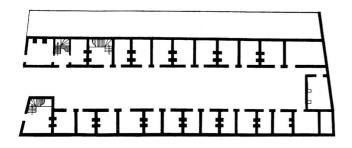

A court in Birmingham. The houses nearest the open end or facing the street were slightly better.

SANITATION

Sanitation was virtually non-existent in these small houses. Water was not 'laid on', nor were there any proper sewers. Water had to be collected by hand from a nearby source – a well, spring or pump.

The privy was at the end of the yard for the throughs. For the back-to-backs, its position varied. It might stand against a boundary wall or be situated in the middle of the yard. In a court there was often a block of privies situated against a side wall.

DUST AND ASH

Each family produced about two tons of ash each year.

Access to the yard or back for dustmen and nightmen was of crucial importance. If it was difficult, serious health problems could ensue.

THE BOTTOM LINE

Back-to-backs could be built for as little as £70–£90 each, though only relatively large-scale developments could get the cost down this far. High demand invariably meant higher rents.

The rent for a back-to-back varied between 1s 6d and 3s a week, depending on demand. A mill hand earning 21s a week would be lucky to find a back-to-back for as little as 1s 6d. If local demand was high, he might have to share with another family and pay just as much.

The rent of a through house was usually one-quarter to one-third more than that of a back-to-back and was, of course, equally affected by the state of the housing market.

During this period employers needed to attract workers and became actively involved in building houses.

As larger workforces were required, with employees being numbered in hundreds, so building operations also grew in scale.

Dust and refuse collectors had a hard job keeping the dwellings salubrious.

LATE GEORGIAN 1774-1810

EPILOGUE

A COMPLETE SOCIAL RANGE

For the first time, a complete range of town housing existed for all those who could make ends meet. The same principles of design, layout and construction applied across the range. Brick or stone walls, sash windows, parapet wall and slate roof contained a basic layout of one room behind the other. It was an economical and, by the end of the eighteenth century, a well-known formula. And it was in demand, a growing demand which was fuelled by a growing population and a growing economy which was transforming Britain into an industrial nation.

URBAN CLASSES

There was a further significant development during the late Georgian period. Under the London Building Act of 1774, 'mechanics', tradesmen, merchants and nobility were identified by *the size of the houses in which they lived*. Previous perceptions of society had their basis in concepts such as land ownership and crafts. The identification of town dwellers by the size of their houses represented a significant change of perception.

Large

Medium

Small

REGENCY & EARLY VICTORIAN 1811–50

The Prince Regent

The Regency period was named after the Prince Regent, who was both patron and trendsetter. The architectural style which began during the Regency lasted until the middle of the nineteenth century.

Regency style evolved from the late Georgian, specifically that of Robert Adam. Whole estates in this style were planned and built for the top end of the housing market. The sheer weight and presence of these buildings is still remarkable today.

HEALTH, WEALTH AND THE SEASIDE

The Prince Regent made Brighton popular as a fashionable and healthy place where wealthy people might stay. In the wake of Brighton came numerous other seaside developments. These seaside resorts were the fastest growing towns of the first half of the nineteenth century.

The Royal Pavilion in Brighton was both fashionable and exotic in style.

CONTINUING URBANISATION

It was becoming increasingly fashionable for polite society to live in towns. At the same time, towns were developing as centres of commerce and industry and attracting more and more of the population. The population itself continued its extraordinary growth. By 1811, Britain was an industrial nation without any real competition from abroad.

Polite society took care to live in a different part of town to the areas of production. The middle class were anxious to follow suit.

A NEW STYLE

Carlton House Terrace, designed by Nash for the Prince Regent.

The demand for urban housing stimulated architects and builders like John Nash, James Burton and Thomas Cubitt into wholesale production of houses for the top end of the market – those in easy, or at least comfortable, circumstances.

A new style of large houses emerged. The urban form was the large terraced house. A giant by comparison with its Georgian predecessor, Regency terraces were often grander than nearby public buildings and continued to be a success for very many years. Their upper-class clientele didn't mind rubbing shoulders with socially acceptable neighbours. The occupants enjoyed far more space, privacy, comfort and also a higher standard of hygiene than their continental equivalents in Paris or Vienna.

French and German writers commented upon this. Cesar Daly, a French critic, called the large Regency terraced house 'the most functional design...with servants in the attic and coal in the cellars'.

HOW DID THE REGENCY HOUSE DIFFER?

The large Regency house contained more rooms but was not significantly wider than its Georgian equivalent. It was simply taller. Additional rooms were accommodated by adding more storeys: fourth, fifth and even sixth floors. This affected the overall classical proportions. Classical principles were applied to parts of the house as well as the whole, and individual features, such as windows, were emphasised. The facade itself was sub-divided by accentuating horizontals such as the cornice. Centre and end blocks of up-market terraces continued to be salient features. For large and medium-sized houses, it was the appearance and proportion of particular features that maintained the principles of classicism. For small houses, it was a different story altogether.

Cumberland Terrace, designed by Nash for the very top end of the market.

NEW AND EXOTIC INFLUENCES

Fortunes were being made in India and the 'colonies', and with them new and exotic cultural influences were arriving. Enhanced knowledge of classical antiquity fuelled appetites for the bright and colourful. There was a shift in taste away from Roman towards ancient Greek forms.

Meanwhile, other building developments were taking place in the suburbs.

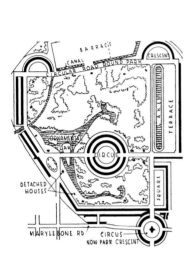

Left: Nash's plan for Regent's Park. The solid blocks were terraces. Note the isolated villas. Above: new and exotic influences – cupolas, battlements, gables and verandahs.

THE VILLA SUBURB

One scheme built in the 1820s, St John's Wood, London, introduced the idea of the 'villa suburb' – areas of gracious, detached houses standing in their own grounds on the outskirts of town. As a speculation, St John's Wood was not a resounding success. The anticipated 'Villa Boom' did not materialise. But St John's Wood was to be the prototype of similar developments on the healthier outskirts of towns whose centres were becoming overcrowded and unhealthy.

Below left: Estate plan of an early villa suburb, very low density housing to which the occupants of the centre of town could only aspire. Below right: a Regency villa designed by Nash.

LARGE – *front*

A LIGHTER LOOK

Regency houses followed the same design as the late Georgian, but the execution was a lighter and less rigid interpretation of the principles of classicism. The strict rules of Palladianism were not entirely abandoned, but gave way to more graceful, harmonious Greek forms. 'Fluidity' was brought into the design.

WHAT WAS DIFFERENT?

Houses became larger – more storeys were added. Some houses had fifth and even sixth floors. A half-basement replaced the full basement, creating a grander, more imposing facade and also saving the builder the cost of extensive excavation.

MORE DECORATIVE DETAIL

Stucco began to be used much more extensively on ground-floor walls, and for decorative pilasters, architraves and cornices.

In this period, people liked looking at what was going on in the street. Cast iron enabled balconies to be built, running the width of the building and around the bow windows, on the first floor. The most fashionable and prevalent patterns were the heart and honeysuckle motifs. Ironwork was usually painted a turquoisy green to resemble the patina of antiqued bronze.

These balconies or elaborate tablatures took the place of the modest Georgian string course. From the 1830s, French windows/doors often replaced the large sash windows on the first floor.

In keeping with the original concept of the terrace, all the houses in it were painted the same colour.

Centre and end-of-terrace blocks were given additional emphasis by the use of columns, a design feature that lasted until the 1840s.

52 ft
15.8 m

24 ft
7.3 m

Large terraced house with stuccoed cornice concealing junction of roof and wall. At first-floor level: stuccoed course, ironwork balcony and French doors. Large panes of glass were used instead of the smaller Georgian ones. Steps lead up to the front door, the basement being, in effect, a half-basement.

End section of a terrace showing giant columns, a feature that went out of fashion for new buildings after 1840.

Side view of an end-of-terrace house.

Bow windows: 'to see the sea'. The ultimate development of this feature was to build the entire front of each house as a bow.

A villa design linked to its neighbours by a party wall on one side and its entrance 'wing' on the other.

LETTING THE OUTSIDE IN

Double doors between rooms became more common and they were left open so you could see from the front to the back. Two rooms thus became one. Large sashes or French windows led directly on to balconies, verandahs or conservatories. This created a marriage of the interior with the exterior. Large mirrors – which reflected the light and the foliage, particularly at the front – created an illusion of light and space, letting the outside in.

These changes were all part of the spirit of opening up the house, breaking the rigid lines of the Georgian design, allowing in more light and also the outside, in the verdant form it took in front of the best Regency houses (the square, crescent etc. and the garden at the back). They would put up huge mirrors to catch this light and green fancy and throw it back into the room.

REGENCY COLOUR

New discoveries about antiquity brought the knowledge that the ancient Greeks used to paint the exteriors of their buildings and statues.

The use of stucco to imitate stone also had a considerable effect on Regency exteriors. They were altogether brighter and more vivid than their Georgian forebears.

However, the fashionable stone to imitate was the sandy Bath colour, even if the 'local' stone was another hue entirely, such as the light grey Portland.

Other external details also came in for a more colourful treatment. Railings and ironwork were painted green mixed with powdered copper to give them an antique bronze effect.

Front doors were always painted in a dark colour, unless they were made of mahogany or oak.

THOMAS CUBITT

Some builders were spectacularly successful. Thomas Cubitt began as a carpenter, made a fortune, enjoyed the patronage of Queen Victoria and transformed the practices of the building industry itself.

Cubitt was an innovator. He hired his own craftsmen and then kept them on from job to job. To keep his men busy between commissions, he took on more and more speculative work. He preferred to work at the top end of the market, building large terraced houses on aristocratically-owned estates. Eventually Cubbitt built a wing of Buckingham Palace and also Osborne House, Queen Victoria's retreat on the Isle of Wight.

LARGE – *plan*

CHANGES IN PLAN DOWNSTAIRS

Changes, substantial ones, were all located towards the rear.

The kitchen was moved out of the main body of the house into a large rear extension to avoid the 'fry and fat smell' in the reception rooms. A new service room appeared – the scullery. The piped water supply was located there and washing became separated from cooking. More space was now available at this level for other servants' rooms.

UPSTAIRS

The basic plan of the main house remained the same – the drawing room was still on the first floor, etc.

Many more bedrooms were added, which gave girls and boys of this class separate bedrooms. The families also employed more servants and they too needed accommodation.

As the rear extension became larger, it provided a third main room for the family on the ground and first floors. This additional space was used for different functions depending on the household; in many houses it provided dressing rooms for master and mistress.

RENT

Over the same period annual rents increased to one tenth of the building cost. Houses like these could cost as much as £1,000 to build. Correspondingly, the rent would be £50–£100 a year.

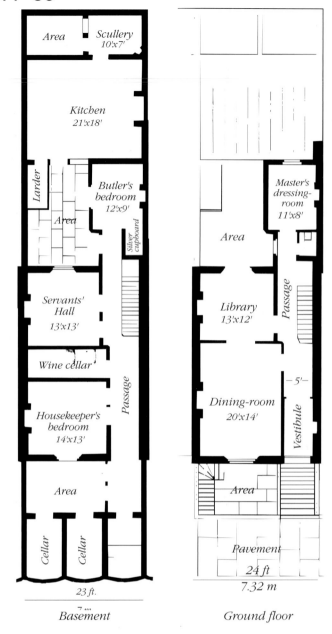

Basement

Ground floor

Bedroom furniture: note the skirting board and draperies.

Letting the outside in.

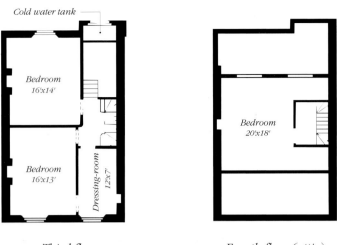

Cold water tank

Bedroom
16'x14'

Bedroom
16'x13'

Dressing-room
12'x7'

Third floor

Bedroom
20'x18'

Fourth floor (attic)

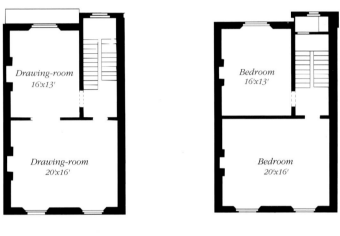

Drawing-room
16'x13'

Drawing-room
20'x16'

First floor

Bedroom
16'x13'

Bedroom
20'x16'

Second floor

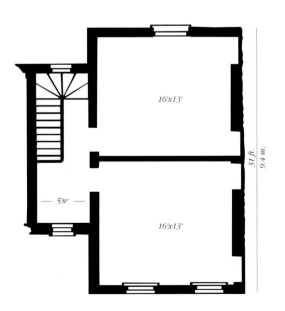

16'x13'

16'x13'

31 ft.
9.4 m.

5'8"

Plan of ground floor of semi-detached house.

WHO LIVED IN THEM?

The people who lived in these large houses of fourteen or so rooms belonged to the upper echelons of society: those of 'independent' means and the upper middle class, top professionals and those who had become rich through commerce and industry.

The cost of building was in the process of doubling between 1790 and 1840, chiefly because the new houses were so much larger but also because land values rose in response to the demand.

CALLING CARDS

Calling cards played a vital role in the life of a society that required written notice of an intended visit. Cards might be delivered by a footman, but common practice was to carry several cards in a case.

Fashionable ladies eager to impress others would display cards presented to them by notable visitors in a large open dish placed on the drawing-room table.

Visitors of note were, of course, received in the drawing-room on the first floor. It was considered impolite to pay a social call before midday.

Unless they had been invited to dine, visitors would be offered light refreshments, such as tea, cake and sandwiches.

LADY DEVENISH

1 REGENCY TERRACE
THE FASHIONABLE PART OF TOWN

A drawing-room scene early in the Regency period.

LARGE – *back*

MEWS AND REAR EXTENSIONS

Like the Georgian, the back of the large Regency terrace house still meant services. Nearby were a cluster of mews, back-courts and 'mean streets', which were a necessary adjunct to a genteel neighbourhood.

In London and Brighton houses, the rear extensions shared a wall with their mews where the horses, vehicles, grooms and coachmen were accommodated. Elsewhere, the mews was situated nearby.

The mews was noticeably lower than the street level at the front of the house, which was 'made up'.

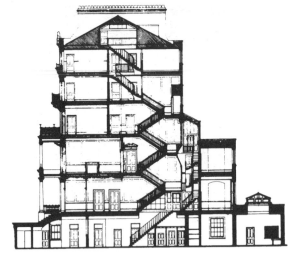

Cross-section from the front (left) to the rear extensions, including the kitchen but not the mews. Back stairs and kitchen skylight are clearly visible.

Key to main illustration:

1. Dormer windows to attic rooms

2. Extension to accommodate back stairs

3. Conservatory

4. Rear extension, accommodating additional main rooms

5. Rear areas

6. Pantry

7. WC

8. Butler's bedroom with silver cupboard

9. Kitchen

10. Scullery

11. Stables

12. Stables

13. Coachman or groom or hayloft

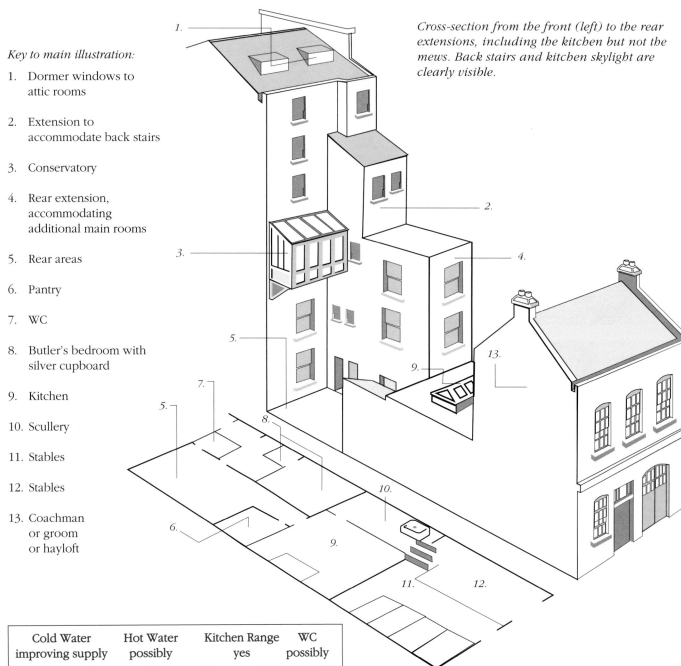

Cold Water improving supply	Hot Water possibly	Kitchen Range yes	WC possibly

Carriage-folk with their attendant grooms and coachmen.

Mews buildings retained the earlier plain styling. The large doors were for the horses and carriages.

A busy mews in the 1840s.

THE SERVANT HIERARCHY

Upper

female	male
Lady's maid	Butler
Housekeeper	Valet
Cook	
	Nanny*
Nursery maid	

The nanny ranked highest, even with a butler in the house. A butler was replaceable. A good nanny was not.

Lower

Chambermaid	Footman
Housemaid	Boy
Laundry maid	
Maid of all work	
Scullery maid	

Maid of all work   Butler

Housemaid

47

MEDIUM – *front*

EMULATION OF THE LARGE

The medium-sized house emulated the large in as many ways as it could. However, it was difficult for the medium to retain much of the classical proportions apart from the width/height formula of the windows and their placement.

The main features copied from the large houses were the half basement, use of stucco and decorative ironwork.

The ground floor was elevated and the steps and area protected by iron railings. The larger-scale production of cast iron meant that more elaborate patterns were available at a lower price.

Instead of the Georgian plain brick parapet, a more elaborate cornice was introduced.

ROOFS

Tiles were going out of fashion and slates becoming more and more common on pitched roofs. Many Regency houses had a flat roof which was covered in lead.

SKYLINE

Design stopped at the roof of the house and all urban skylines were cluttered with chimneys.

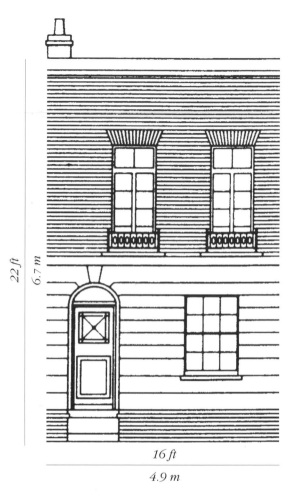

22 ft
6.7 m

16 ft
4.9 m

Half-basement, stucco and ironwork emulated that of the large.

Terrace to which the individual house shown above belonged.

Another arrangement of the facade: Entrances combined and recessed; paired fronts combined under a single gable.

Ironwork porch, awning and ground floor
balconet embellish this example.

An elegant solution to the problem of
aligning ground floor windows.

THE PREVIOUS PERIOD'S BEST

The Regency medium received the innovations that the Georgian large had enjoyed. These houses were also larger and more expensive than their Georgian predecessors.

MULTIPLE OCCUPATION

Most of the original occupants were better off than their predecessors, too. In some areas, there was either little smaller accommodation or a lack of strong control by the landlord. This class of housing might then be occupied by more than one family. Usually this led to the deterioration of both the property and the street, or even the neighbourhood.

WHO OWNED THEM?

As medium-sized developments were altogether on a smaller scale than their larger relations, they were often less well managed. This inevitably resulted in them going down-market.

Well-managed properties were let on strict conditions. The most vital of these were no sub-letting and no trade or industrial activity. If there was any kind of industry nearby, such as soap or candle-making, a brewery or a tannery, the entire neighbourhood could lose its social pretensions and the landlords' profit margin was substantially reduced.

AS SAFE AS HOUSES

Building and developing were risky, but investing in building was safe. Much of the capital for small housing was put up by the middle class. By and large, they preferred this relatively safe form of investment.

Building investment brought a return of four and a half to five per cent, which was usually a bit better than Government stock and one to two per cent less than more risky ventures like railways. The capital was often invested through their solicitor. It was thought to be 'as safe as houses'.

Modest houses such as these might have been occupied by more than one family.

MEDIUM – *plan*

CHANGES IN PLAN

The most common change in plan of the medium-sized house resulted from the addition of a small rear extension. In the basement, this accommodated the new scullery with its recently installed supply of piped water. At ground level, it provided a 'retiring room' or closet.

The kitchen moved to the back, closer to the water supply. In some houses the front basement room was used as a sitting-room or breakfast-room by the family, but in those which still had the piano nobile it was used by the servants.

The average ceiling height became one foot higher than the Georgian equivalent, as it did in the larger houses.

REGENCY AVERAGES

Average population per house in 1821: 5.75.

By 1814, the average rent had doubled since 1790. This reflected the increase in size of the houses and the rise in building costs. A medium-sized Regency house with five to six main rooms cost £16–£26 per annum to rent.

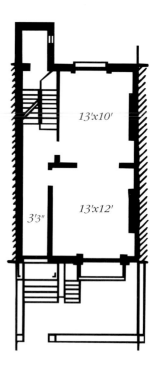

Ground floor of a house with a small rear (closet) extension.

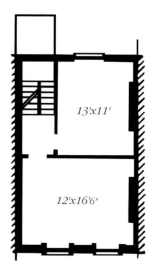

First floor of a house with a small rear (closet) extension.

Modest Regency interiors with carpets, curtains on pole rails and hooks in the ceilings for hanging lamps or candelabra.

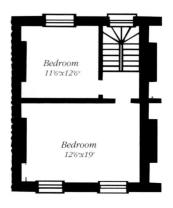

Second floor belonging to plans shown opposite.

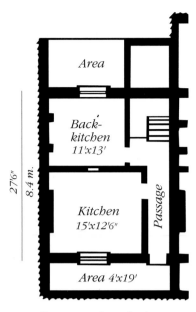

*Basement plan of a house
without a closet wing.*

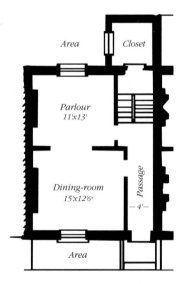

*Ground-floor plan of a house
without a closet wing.*

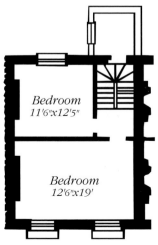

First-floor plan.

FIREPLACES

Just as the hierarchy of parts of the house was exhibited on the outside by the placing of decorative features, the social boundaries in the house were reflected by the decorating and furnishing of the rooms. Fireplaces were an interesting guide to the importance of a room.

The best room would normally have a marble fireplace – after that, slate would be a common material. In the bedrooms they were usually smaller and made of cast iron. In the servants' quarters, the fireplace would be smaller still, with a plain wood surround.

COAL AND SOOT

The new closed kitchen ranges, or kitcheners, used one ton of coal every forty days. It has been estimated that an entire ton of soot from unburnt coal dust fell on every area of twenty-five square miles.

A substantial part of middle-class incomes had to be spent on the home just to keep it salubrious. Of course, there were numerous other bills the householder had to pay apart from the rent and the servants' wages.

THE BURDEN OF BILLS

Income tax had arrived to stay during the Napoleonic War. The famous window tax appears to have been a kind of predecessor to the Rates, providing income for local government.

The medium houses began to receive piped water supplies, but these were sufficiently expensive for the water companies to offer a cheaper alternative at a lower pressure. Householders could choose between either High or Low pressure supplies. It could cost as much as 3s a week.

DODGY GAS

The middle class were as yet rather wary of gas lighting in their homes. Gas, too, was still rather expensive at 15s per cubic foot.

A TYPICAL PROFILE

In 1843, a particular diamond merchant lived in a four-bedroom, two-reception room house in London. The house had a kitchen in the basement. With him lived his wife, a maiden aunt, five children and two live-in servants. He probably walked the five miles to work. His income would have been between £300–£400. To support such an establishment required between one-quarter and one third of his income.

MEDIUM – *back*

INCONVENIENCE

The back of the medium-sized house accommodated the usual services. Sometimes the only access was through the house, which would have been a great inconvenience to its inhabitants who were trying to maintain appearances.

Ash and coals were still being heaped at the back. Sewage was now possibly connected to the drains where it became somebody else's problem, but the backs of the houses still smelt.

GUTTERING

Roof gutters and run-off pipes became a standard feature in most new houses and this enabled people to experiment with a variety of water closets. Better down-pipes and hoppers were affordable because they were made of cast iron. These were only visible at the rear of the house as the run of the gutter was from front to back.

Gravel covering of the yard still had to be raked every few days as it became blackened by soot.

Cold Water	Hot Water	Kitchen Range	WC
improving supply	no	possibly	possibly

View of the back, showing the lead roof of the rear extension used as a terrace and a privy. This example actually has a garden; many mediums of this period did not.

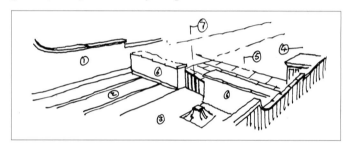

1	Boundary wall	4	Skylight to back kitchen
2	Lead roof or rear	5	Privy in outhouse
	extension used as a	6	Paved area
	terrace	7	Steps to paved area
3	Parapet		

The other extreme: houses backing on to streams or ditches which had become open sewers.

Another interior from this period shows carpet and curtains, hanging lamp, pictures and wall sconces.

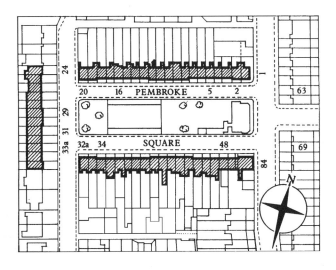

Medium-sized houses built on a well laid out estate. The norm for mediums of this period was more cramped at the rear and lacked the garden in the square.

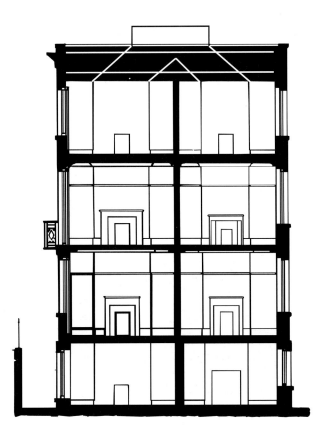

Cross-section shows location of main kitchen had moved to the rear of the basement; drawing-room was still on the first floor, so space remaining for bedrooms was limited.

THE REAR EXTENSION ARRIVES

The rear extension was introduced to the medium-sized house to contain the new water closet. Like the water tap, it was located at the back. The kitchen moved towards it, which allowed the possibility of the front basement room being used as a less formal reception room. This arrangement suited the smaller mediums.

LARGER DIMENSIONS

On average, the medium houses had ceilings one foot higher than previously.

In common with the general pattern, they tended to have one fewer fireplace than they had main rooms. A house with two reception rooms, four bedrooms and a kitchen would have had six fireplaces. The smallest bedroom would have been the room that missed out.

OTHER DETAILS

Fireplaces, by contrast, grew smaller. They were more efficient, having a smaller opening. In a medium, they were probably made of cast iron and blacked. The surround was possibly made of artificial 'Coade' stone, plaster or pine. In the latter case, the surround was probably painted.

The stairs might have had cast-iron newel posts. The main rooms would have had fitted carpets or at the least a floorcloth, known as a 'drugget', painted green.

A rather utilitarian reception room: visitors are being received and a meal has been laid on the table at the back.

SMALL – *front*

ERA OF ABUSE

Small houses at this time were often built on small parcels of land that were sold off to different builders. The result was almost always a lack of proper development of the street – in effect, no street at all.

The houses were built so densely that proper sanitation, drainage and ventilation were non-existent. There might be more than one hundred houses per acre.

This dense building created blind courts and, in turn, this spread epidemic diseases.

SAME DESIGN – MORE PROBLEMS

Externally, the smallest houses still basically resembled the largest of the Georgian period. This was due to the standards imposed by the earlier building acts and also to the availability of pattern books on style to every level of the building trade.

The original design of the small house remained sound, but enormous problems were created when too many houses were packed into limited spaces. This was caused by the greed of speculators who were providing all the housing now that employers no longer had to lure workers to the city with ready-built homes.

There was also local opposition from landowners who either refused to lease their land for building or opposed development in general. The result was overcrowding. Most small urban houses now contained more than one family.

When first built, these small houses were described as working-men's cottages.

In the West Midlands it was common for two houses to share a common entrance. Access to the individual houses was from a tunnel, which led from the street to the yards at the back.

Front elevation of two pairs of back-to-backs (Manchester) showing the tunnel entrance to the court (centre).

Unpaved streets, without drains or main sewers, were further fouled by stagnant water, dunghills and even pigsties; all overlooked by nearby heavy industry (in this case, a gasworks).

There was very little stylistic change to small houses. This terrace has been given some Regency touches: stucco, window surrounds, a course at first-floor level and the doors have rectangular fanlights. In all other respects, the design does not differ from the earlier Georgian. Such houses were usually occupied by several families.

The front of a small house in Manchester showing the steps leading down to the cellar.

A squalid cellar dwelling. Immigrants from the countryside continued to keep livestock in towns.

THE WORKING CLASSES

By the 1830s, the workforces of the textile, coal and iron industries were being referred to as the 'working classes'. They ranged from unskilled labourer to skilled artisan. They had regular jobs, as opposed to those below them on the social scale, who relied on day-to-day employment for their livelihood.

IMMMIGRANT WORKERS

People walked into the towns from the nearby country, looking for work. They could earn 21s a week from mill-work, as opposed to 13s 6d on the land, supposing work was available. It was the difference between having or not having a piece of beef to put between your pieces of bread.

These new arrivals intensified the demand for housing because the existing population of the town was itself growing.

DEMAND FOR LAND

There was a need for new building land. In response, both existing sites and new ones were developed. The new were usually small parcels of land between the existing urban areas. This linked up existing urban agglomerations and created large industrial areas.

The demand for new housing was met almost entirely by speculators who had recognised that the rent from small houses could be profitable. A large pool of houses and labour came into being. Only the largest scale industries needed to attract the highly skilled by providing accommodation.

SHODDY BUILDING

However, the potential for only a low rent led to shoddy building. Although the dimensions of the houses were predetermined, the materials and workmanship were of the lowest kind.

In order to realise any profit, builders skimped in their work – a practice which had earlier been forced upon them by the inflated price of land and materials due to the Napoleonic Wars (1793–1814). Building costs in this time had almost doubled.

Unfortunately, they continued to do it as long as they could get away with it. During this period there was virtually nothing to stop them.

Courts built during the Regency period.

SMALL – *plan*

AN ALL-TIME LOW

Houses were built for as little as £54 each, an all-time low.

Even in stone areas, brick was used for chimney stacks and party walls as it became cheaper. Slate was the most common roofing material.

SHRINKAGE

Back-to-backs became even smaller than their Georgian equivalents. Building society statistics collected in the mid-century show that the most numerous type had a cellar, living-room and single bedroom. It had neither convenience nor any water supply – other than a rain-water barrel. The privy was usually shared with many other homes.

In very bad areas there was no drainage and only an unpaved horse road in front, which could be one foot deep in mud. There might also be stagnant water. The worst areas were the crowded, filthy yards and cellars.

The newly built back-to-backs were not only smaller but less soundly constructed then their predecessors.

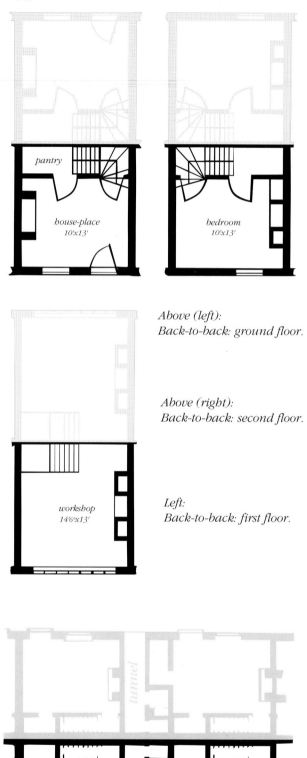

Above (left):
Back-to-back: ground floor.

Above (right):
Back-to-back: second floor.

Left:
Back-to-back: first floor.

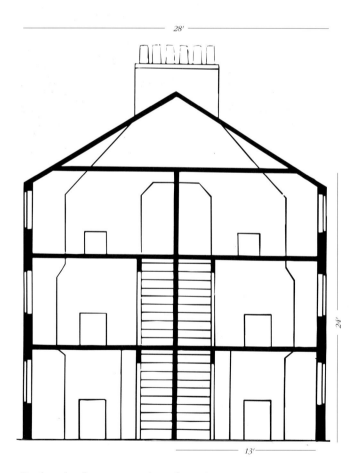

Back-to-backs: cross-section of a pair.

Plan of back-to-backs showing tunnel to the court; the toilets were entered from the tunnel. The space above was occupied by a bedroom (Manchester).

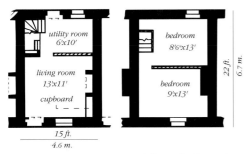

Through house: Ground floor (left) and first floor (right).

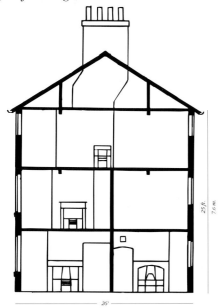

Cross-section of a through house (Nottingham).

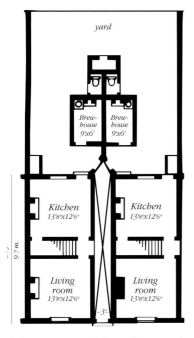

Through houses entered from the tunnel, typical of the West Midlands. Sculleries and toilets were in the yard. The sculleries were equipped with set-pots and were referred to as 'brew-houses'.

OVERCROWDING

In 1839, there were records of six people to a room and ten people in a house. This was representative of conditions in the bad areas, and they were numerous.

MORTALITY RATES

At the end of the period, mortality rates as high as 21.8 per thousand were recorded

JERRY BUILDING

The expression 'jerry building' originated during this period. It came from 'jury-rig', a nautical expression for temporary repairs to rigging, masts and sails. In practice, it meant fast, careless work that skimped on materials to save a few pennies.

Jerry building: the expression first appeared during this era. It was thought that if you didn't skimp on materials and quality you were unlikely to make money out of small houses.

HOUSES THAT HAVE SURVIVED

Only a few small houses from this period have survived. These would have housed the relatively affluent; for example the 'whitesmiths' – the local butcher or baker.

Whitesmiths: relatively affluent occupants of the through houses.

SMALL – *back*

OVERCROWDING

Rent was £4–£7 per annum, representing seventeen to twenty per cent of the family income. It was collected weekly.

Records from 1839 show over six people per room, with an average of ten people per house.

CLOSED COURTS

Courts were originally intended to have an open side, but speculators anxious to 'pack 'em in' succumbed to the temptation to build across the open side. This effectively 'closed' the court.

The only access was by means of a narrow tunnel. This might be as little as three feet wide. The tunnel opened out into a yard which was the only space available for ash and privies. It might also be inhabited by livestock.

EPIDEMICS

Even through houses had problems with lack of rear access to their yards. The accumulation of filth of all kinds acted as a magnet for epidemic diseases, especially the waterborne ones such as cholera and typhus, which swept through these crowded areas.

Cold Water	Kitchen Range	WC
highly unlikely	no	no

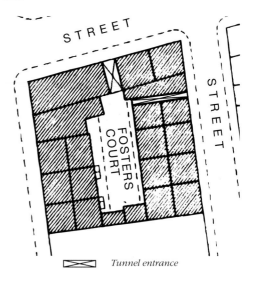

Plan of a closed court: Entrance to the houses on the inside of the court had to be through the tunnels.

☒ *Tunnel entrance*

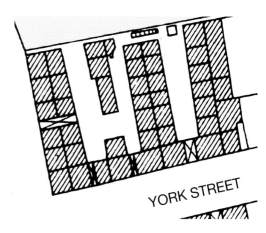

Another court plan requiring tunnel entrances. The industrial building at the top of the plan effectively closed the court.

Left: Illustration of the cramped and crowded conditions created by piecemeal development of urban plots of land. The wall on the left marks the boundary of the property. Not only did this cramp the inhabitants but the dwellings appeared to be overlooked by taller buildings, depriving them of much light or fresh air.

Below right: 'In the court of King Cholera', a near contemporary depiction of the conditions in a crowded court where muck and filth accumulated creating lethal health hazards.

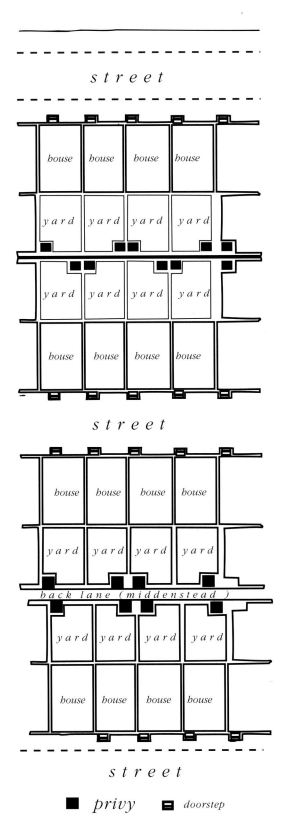

street

street

street

■ *privy*   ▭ *doorstep*

Plans of houses showing how the access to the rear was restricted. Top: Although these houses are equipped with a yard, they had no rear access at all. The houses in the lower plan had a narrow lane or middenstead at the rear, but access to the yards was still difficult and hygiene problems were inevitable.

PIECEMEAL DEVELOPMENT

The principal cause of the problem was piecemeal development: small parcels of land sold off to different builders meant no proper street layout. Sanitation, drainage and adequate ventilation were almost impossible when there was no distinction between the front of a dwelling and the back. It was quite impossible when there were more than a hundred houses per acre.

Local landowners were reluctant to allow their land to be developed for this kind of housing. Land was still 'parcelled off', even when outlying plots became available.

INFILL

Worst of all was the incredibly dense 'infill' of existing urban areas. Older properties were pulled down after the occupants had moved out to a more salubrious area. Numerous dwellings were then built on the site of what had been a single property and then more were built over what had been the yard.

Worst of all, this infill prevented any proper street layout, which made proper drainage impossible and rubbish and ash removal extremely difficult.

LIVESTOCK

Many of the factory workers were newly arrived in town and brought their country habits with them. Seeking an inexpensive way to supplement their diet, they crowded their already tiny backyards with pigsties, hen roosts, pigeon cotes and, in some cases, a small stable.

These animals happily consumed the vegetable waste, but at the same time created an evil-smelling quagmire with all the attendant health problems in hot weather.

An unwelcome visit from the rent collector. This distressed family was occupying the top floor, identifiable by its wide, loomshop windows. These were originally intended to give a better light for working.

EPILOGUE

LARGE

At the top end of the market, houses had changed considerably. They were larger and enjoyed numerous comforts and conveniences their Georgian predecessors had not. They had changed stylistically, yet were still classical in principle.

The period had seen many new designs, ideas and developments, some of which were really waiting in the wings for adoption later on a large scale. The villa suburb, in particular, was the advance guard of an altogether larger development to come.

MEDIUM

The medium emulated the large as much as it could. The trickle down effect granted the medium the benefits only available to the large in the Georgian period.

SMALL

Not so the small, whose lot had changed not for the better but for the worse. Increased demand and higher land values caused by rapid urbanisation had made rents rise.

The newly-named 'working classes' were actually paying more for less. Despite the economic growth of the period, only a small proportion of working-class people enjoyed better housing during this period.

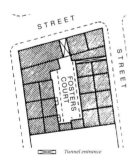

Tunnel entrance

PUBLIC CONCERN

The lack of regulation and proper control of the preceding half century resulted in considerable public concern. This was further fuelled by the cholera epidemics of the 1830s and 1840s.

Population increases had contributed to both labour troubles and epidemic diseases – most notably waterborne diseases, which spread rapidly in the overcrowded areas. The epidemics, in particular, affected everyone.

The reaction was twofold – first, a broadly based reform movement, and second, the widely felt desire to move out of the overcrowded, unhealthy urban centre.

MID-VICTORIAN 1851—75

Queen Victoria was the longest reigning monarch of all – from 1837 to 1901 – but a distinctive Victorian style only really emerged across the board after the middle of the century.

PERIOD OF IMPROVEMENT

During the Mid-Victorian period, Britain retained its lead over potential industrial rivals. Europe was in turmoil and the United States was concentrating on the opening up of the West and its Civil War. At home and abroad Britain enjoyed increased prosperity. The benefits became apparent in the newly built homes of all three classes. Thankfully, the preceding 'period of abuse' was followed by a period of improvement.

A view of the Great Exhibition.

Political reform resulted in larger and more organised local government. It was up to these new local officials to implement the rulings regarding sanitation, water supply and other public services. They were not altogether successful, although in some cases the public outcry was so great that considerable improvement took place.

VICTORIAN VALUES

Victorian values stressed home and nation at the expense of neighbourhood and community. This was admirably expressed in the Great Exhibition of 1851 when over 15,000 products were exhibited – great numbers of them for the home or for the building of homes.

INVENTIONS

The period was also the great age of inventions, both on a national and domestic scale. The second generation of Victorians wholeheartedly embraced and adopted new products and 'mod cons' for their homes. Ready-made items and cheaper, better materials were constantly appearing. These were often promoted on a national basis by both advertising and catalogues.

A new letterbox, one of innumerable inventions and innovations which affected house and home.

VICTORIAN STYLE

John Ruskin

The second generation of Victorians reacted against the style of the preceding generation. The contemporary authority on art, John Ruskin, referred to the classicism of the Regency terraces as 'drab uniformity'.

Classical forms remained popular, particularly among the establishment, but a greater variety of alternatives became evident, appearing alongside the classical in large numbers. Classical and the alternatives all developed a distinctive Victorian form. The proponents of each form maintained that theirs was not only the most attractive but also, in some way, morally superior.

ECLECTICISM

A rustic Italian form became popular. This was based on the Tuscan villa designs of the Renaissance period. Osborne House, Queen Victoria's new summer home on the Isle of Wight, made the form both respectable and fashionable.

A little later another form was adopted by the speculative builders: Gothic. This form of Gothic was far more than the mere medieval dressings on classical frames which had passed for 'Gothic' previously.

Despite their distinctive differences, the Classical, Italian and Gothic forms shared a number of common features which united them into an overall style. This Victorian style was the first heterogeneous, or eclectic style.

The Houses of Parliament – a major showpiece of the Gothic form.

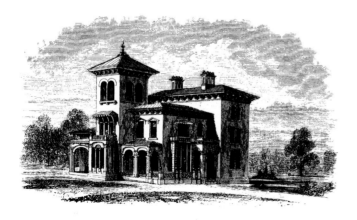

A villa design in the Rustic Italian form.

A cottage design in the Gothic form.

The new style had its greatest impact in the rapidly expanding suburbs. These suburbs grew as a result of the second phase of railway development from the 1850s onwards. The new railways formed networks of suburban lines leading to termini in the town centres.

Housing developers and railway companies worked closely together. Housing estates grew up around local stations where land values were less high than in existing urban areas. Areas which had merely been dotted with Regency villas were gradually filled in by row upon row of medium-sized houses. For the first time, dense single-class areas of medium-sized houses were created. The lower rents more than compensated for the cost of the fare.

Work place and home were drawing further apart. Eager to benefit from cleaner air, more space and better services, the middle class moved outwards. The pattern was first set in the south-east and followed throughout the country.

Left: Building the railways.

The expansion of the railways was an integral part of the development of towns and houses.

By 1850, the railways were entering their second generation. This generation was directly responsible for the creation of the suburbs.

Right: Despite the intensive building activity, builders were generally held in low esteem. This 1849 cartoon expressed this opinion.

An army of workmen has arrived as the consequence of a single loose slate.

LARGE – *front*

MULTIPLE FORMS

The striking aspect of 'Victorian' style was its multiplicity of forms. These can be divided into three main groups – the Italian Renaissance, the Gothic and a further development of the established Classical. Builders frequently mixed and matched these forms.

A major change in house fashion was taking place: the terrace was no longer the most predominant type of town housing, as semi-detached and villa designs became common in the new suburbs.

Whatever form the style took, the new architectural feature which they all shared was the canted, or straight-sided, bay window.

CONTINUING CLASSICAL

In place of the defining large pilaster, the Victorian classic emphasised the individual windows, transforming them into miniature temple-like features called aediculae.

The first-floor balcony was extended to form a portico stretching over the front door and out over the steps to the pavement.

Balustrading took the place of ironwork on the balcony and was also used along the parapet as a linking design feature. Brackets appeared under the cornice and corners were picked out by quoining.

GOTHIC

The Gothic style emphasised the vertical and two-dimensional surface decoration – the use of moulded and different-coloured bricks. Gables, bargeboards and brackets were used extensively; details abounded. It embodied a general escape from classicism.

ITALIAN RENAISSANCE

Taking its inspiration from Italy, this form followed the characteristic features of the Renaissance palazzo: projecting eaves with brackets, and pairing of first- and second-floor windows. This finally solved the problem of alignment with the ground-floor window. Exteriors were often brick, to which stucco effects might be added.

Continuing classical front, with bay window, portico and balcony added. The emphasis was on individual features, such as windows and balustrades.

54 ft / 16.5 m

25 ft / 7.6 m

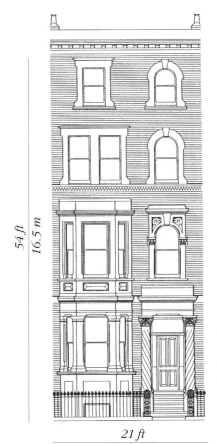

54 ft / 16.5 m

21 ft / 6.4 m

Characteristics of classical, Gothic, Italian and other forms fused together. This sort of fusion was popular with builders and also many occupants.

Section of a classical terrace, featuring unclassical bay windows.

Semi-detached villa in the Italian form, with projecting eaves and windows aligned above each other. The straight-sided bay window became widespread after glass and window taxes were abolished.

Classical cornice, frieze, alignment and aediculae. Second- and third-floor window surrounds have haunches. The bay window and porch are characteristically Victorian.

MORE PEOPLE, MORE MONEY

The Industrial Revolution brought a new wealth, particularly to a rapidly increasing part of the population – the middle classes. Monied and keen to achieve their dream – inspired by those above them – of being the sole occupants of a house and garden of their own, they flocked to the outer edges of the towns where this was possible. The suburbs grew in response. Moving away from the centre achieved many goals: it removed them from the health hazards of life in the city, with its poor sanitation and slums; it gave them the privacy which they valued so highly; and it was also a firm statement of their social aspirations. They could afford to commute because of the improved transportation. The new railway lines, horse-drawn trams, omnibuses and steamboats all brought them from the suburbs into their places of work.

KEEPING UP STANDARDS

The developers initially built suburban housing estates only for the middle classes and tried to keep them as exclusive as possible. The majority of Victorians still rented their houses and a 'high-class' development brought in higher rents. The greatest fear for landlords was that their estate would become run down and they wouldn't be able to get the rents they wanted.

This attitude suited the occupants – whose snobbish aspirations had brought them there in the first place. Neighbours had to be of the same class or better – standards had to be kept up.

FIRST-CLASS FARES

Developers encouraged the railways to offer only first-class fares to their suburban stations and to discourage trains that might be carrying working men from stopping at them. A complex ticket system ensured that the middle-class train commuters never had to share a platform or carriage with working-class passengers.

A 'PRIVATE' ESTATE

Some of the more pretentious estates, which aspired to emulate the upper-class country homes in more than name, actually had lodges (installed with a gatekeeper) built at their entrances. These estates consisted of one or several roads, and their semi-privacy was ensured by gates which were often closed at night.

A fashionable part of town in the 1860s.

LARGE – *plan*

THREE DIFFERENT FORMS OF PLAN

There were now three different forms of plan – terrace, semi detached and villa.

The new developments were a complete antithesis to the regimented rows, crescents and squares of the classically inspired housing of the Georgian and Regency periods. The new estates were built on suburban plots of land, which retained existing roads and country lanes.

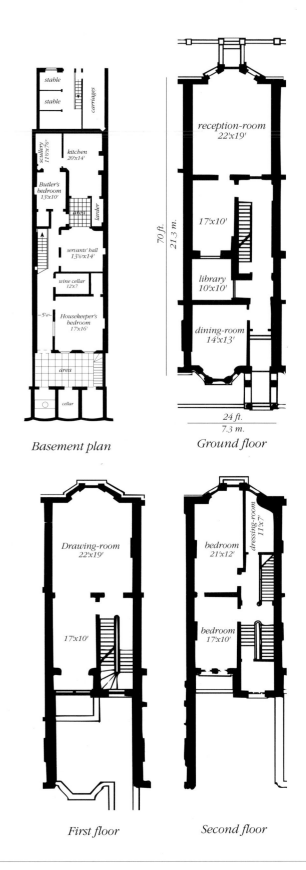

Basement plan   *Ground floor*

First floor   *Second floor*

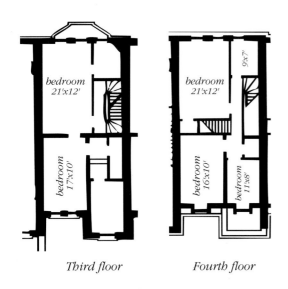

Third floor   *Fourth floor*

Mid-Victorian kitchen lit by skylight and naked gas burners.

The kitchen was situated as far from the main living-room as possible so that 'members, visitors, or guests of the family may not perceive the odour incident to cooking or hear the noise of culinary operations' (Mrs Beeton). The kitchen also had to have a separate access so that servants and tradesmen did not have to pass through the rest of the house. It was moved from the basement to the rear extension.

EXTRA PRIVACY

The only truly private rooms for the Victorian family were their bedrooms and dressing-rooms. It was even recommended that a curtain should be hung in front of bedroom doors for extra privacy, to stop the occupants being caught unawares by servants.

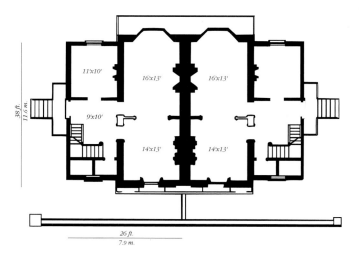

Ground floor of a semi-detached pair of villas with entrances and service rooms at the sides. The results were broader reception rooms (without the need to have them on the piano nobile) and easier access to the back.

Cross-section of a villa design showing bay window, gables and a general movement towards the back and away from the basement. These were all characteristic developments of town houses built during the Mid- and Late-Victorian periods. In this example, the services were located at the back instead of in the basement.

A well-fitted study, a room which usually had a strong masculine feel, as was also usual for the other ground-floor rooms: dining-room and dressing-room.

PRIVACY AND SECLUSION

Whereas during the Regency period people had been outward looking and interested in the life in the street – hence their love of balconies and terraces – the Victorians saw their homes as a haven from the outside world and wanted to shut it out as much as possible. Their focus moved from the community to the family, and their goal was to have space and privacy, elements they could acquire in the suburbs. It was a sign of respectability to live as far away from your work as possible, free from the noise and dirt of commerce.

NOT IN FRONT OF THE SERVANTS

Not only was privacy from the outside world important but also privacy inside the home, and family and servants were kept completely apart. Houses were divided into three disparate parts – the public, private and the unmentionable.

Each particular room had its function and activities were kept completely separate. 'The various

A bedroom c.1865

departments of the household must be distinct, with ready communications by doorways placed wisely to increase privacy' (F. Hooper 1887).

INVISIBLE AND INAUDIBLE

Robert Kerr in *The Gentleman's House* (1864) advocated that *'however small the establishment, the Servants Department shall be separated from the Main House, so that what passes on either side of the boundary shall be both invisible and inaudible on the other'.* This ideal was difficult to carry out in a town house and led to houses being designed with lots of corridors and passageways.

BATHROOM CONVERSIONS

From the 1840s onwards it was possible to pipe hot water throughout the house from a water tank on an upper storey that got its water from the kitchen range. With plumbed-in baths, washbasins and water closets becoming available, people had to find somewhere to put them. The obvious choice was a bedroom or dressing-room.

The new 'bathroom' was furnished no differently from other rooms in the house – it had a fireplace, wall and ceiling mouldings, and wooden floors. Bathroom equipment looked like ordinary furniture. Encasing it in wood ensured that there was no sign of ugly pipes. Walls were covered by dark, heavily patterned wallpaper which didn't show the stains caused by splashmarks and condensation. The room contained a full complement of furniture and bric-à-brac. This usually included cane- or rush-seated chairs, oriental rugs, small tables, wooden-framed mirrors, pictures and prints.

LARGE – *back*

MAJOR DEVELOPMENT

It was now seen as highly desirable to have a garden at the back of the house. This was easily achieved with the villa and the semi-detached plans, but less easy in the new terraces because of the problem of where to put the services. Various schemes were experimented with, such as communal gardens and rear-facing terraces.

The drains and sewage arrangements were improving and therefore more reliable, so odours and spot flooding were less likely. But even in the best houses the problem of the drains were not completely solved yet.

The garden was at the original ground level, as had been the yard. It was therefore necessary to build steps down to it.

The rear elevation or garden front.

A game of battledore, an early form of badminton, being played in the garden.

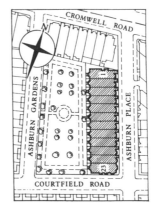

Estate plan showing both garden front and street fronts. The garden was shared, as had been the earlier gardens in the square at the front.

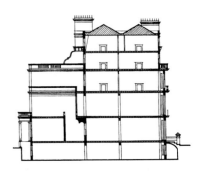

Cross-section of a large terraced house with direct access on to a communal garden.

Cold Water	Hot Water	Kitchen Range	WC	Gas
yes	yes	yes	yes	yes

Above: The garden fronts of suburban villas of a rather Gothic character.

Garden layouts were still formal, with central lawns, bordered by flower-beds and bushes. The far end might be screened by vinery or an arbour as in this example (right).

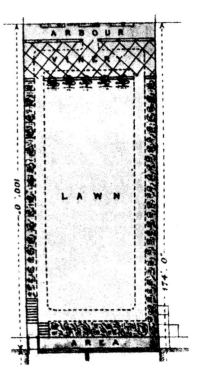

A suburban villa seen from the lawn.

Rustic arch (above). Rusticated garden furniture (right).

Croquet in the garden in 1867.

HOUSE AND GARDEN

The Victorians extended their womb-like attitude to the home to the garden. It was treated as another room of the house. They applied to it their passion for cramming space with objects.

A vast range of ornaments became available, including statues, sundials and vases, in a range of materials from cast iron and imitation marble to artificial stone.

Garden furniture, in keeping with the image of a room, was extremely popular. It was often as elaborate and detailed as the house furniture. People filled their gardens with ornate cast-iron benches, tables and chairs, which were often manufactured in naturalistic shapes such as interwoven branches, ferns, vines and plants. Rusticated furniture was also constructed from unbarked thinnings of wood.

EXOTICA

Frustrated by the corrosive air of London, a Dr Nathaniel Bagshaw Ward had discovered that if plants were sealed in a glass container for long periods of time, they could not only survive, but thrive. He invented the Wardian case, which fitted over a window box. Examples of these can still be seen on some town houses today.

The principle of the Wardian case changed the importation of foreign plants into England. Until its invention, widely-travelling botanists and explorers found their specimens had died en route home. Using the sealed glass container, exotic plants now began to

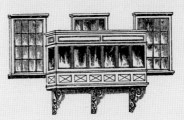

arrive from all corners of the Empire for propagation back in England and rapidly became the vogue in Victorian gardens and conservatories.

The Wardian case

THE CONSERVATORY

Conservatories became ever more popular and they enabled the Victorian house owner to enjoy his exotic flora even in inclement weather. The development and manufacture of cheaper panes of glass, plus advances in producing cast iron, meant that elaborate designs could now be created. The new techniques in heating enabled them to use the conservatory as a room and place to grow exotic plants all through the year.

The conservatories were again highly decorated. Floors consisted of patterned tiles covered with rugs; iron tracery was prevalent; and windows included stained and etched panes. Furniture made of cast iron or wicker often dominated the plants, and any spare space was filled with statues, urns and rock gardens. Caged songbirds were a popular finishing touch.

MEDIUM – *front*

DISTINGUISHING FEATURES

The features which most distinguish the High or Mid-Victorian style are the cant (straight) sided bay, paired front doors and back extensions (see Victorian Medium – plan). Medium-sized houses shared the eclecticism of the style, which was identifiable by these common features despite the various different forms of facade.

BAY WINDOWS

The bay window was designed as a status symbol, but previously there had been numerous obstacles to its adoption in medium-sized houses, namely style and expense. But once the prohibitive window and glass taxes were abolished, it became increasingly available as a standard item. It was doubly welcomed as a way of enlivening facades which had lost any real semblance of Palladian proportion.

THE ITALIAN RENAISSANCE FORM

The Italian Renaissance villa provided a neat solution to the problem of how to align the facade. The characteristic pairing of upper-storey windows aligned comfortably above the bay. Gables, projecting eaves with brackets and round-headed arches for both doors and windows also came from this influence.

A NEW FORM OF CLASSICISM

A form of classicism continued to exist that was quite distinct from the Regency style. This Victorian form consisted of piling on Italianate decorative features and adopting bay windows; features which were anathema to the flat-fronted Palladian tradition. Window alignment generally followed the Italian Renaissance model, although a variation used margin lights to broaden a single window to the width of the bay.

THE GOTHIC FORM

A strong vertical emphasis was the salient feature of the Gothic influence. This was achieved by the use of gables – full or hipped, bargeboards and ridge decorations. Additional decoration was possible in the form of detailed, coloured brickwork. Pointed, lancet windows did not appear as often as squarer, vaguely classical lintels, slim columns and round-headed door arches.

In practice, the builders often hedged their bets and mixed the different forms together.

Right: Flat-fronted house with half-basement, second and attic floors. This type was common in the 1850s, before speculative builders picked up on the bay window as an attractive feature that also solved another longstanding problem: how to align ground- and upper-floor windows on a medium-sized house.

18 ft / 5.5 m
59 ft / 18 m

An example of Gothic form: the lintels and door arch reinforced the vertical emphasis given by the 'cock-roost' dormer window. Note that this example still has a basement. The reputation of basements was declining but they were, as yet, far from disappearing altogether.

15 ft / 4.6 m
28 ft / 8.5 m

Victorian 'classicism': pairing of windows above the bay came from Italian Renaissance form. The window 'columns' were from classical 'stock' mouldings. The bays had full parapets, but eaves were hidden by a half-parapet in the classical manner.

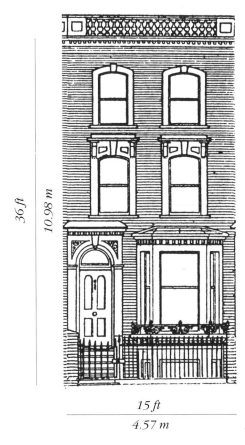

An example built in the late 1860s with a half-basement, bay window and a second storey.

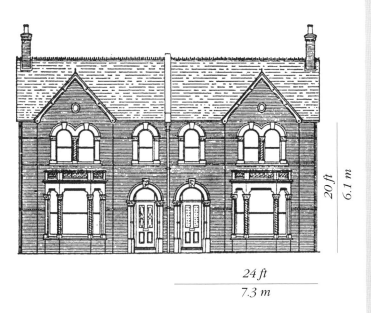

Semi-detached pair faced in a brown brick; the only difference between semi-detached and terrace was the substitution of an end wall instead of a party wall, and a gap of five feet between pairs. This example clearly shows the Italian Renaissance features and the new alignment of the doors and windows.

TAKING THE TRAIN TO WORK

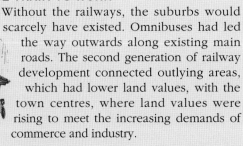

Without the railways, the suburbs would scarcely have existed. Omnibuses had led the way outwards along existing main roads. The second generation of railway development connected outlying areas, which had lower land values, with the town centres, where land values were rising to meet the increasing demands of commerce and industry.

Once the suburban railways acquired termini in the centre of the town, they were able to carry many more passengers to work than the omnibuses and in less time. Down the line, whole developments grew up around the local stations. Branch lines allowed infill. Taking the train to work became the most significant middle-class characteristic.

MIDDLE-CLASS RESPECTABILITY

These suburban areas were also new in that they were socially homogeneous – whole estates of medium-sized houses without any 'mean streets' nearby. The middle class were painfully conscious of their neighbours. Clerks hated rubbing shoulders with tradesmen. Those paying upwards of £50 rent did not want a '£30er' next door. Above all, they cherished the 'respectability' that came from living in a smart house in a good neighbourhood.

WHO WERE THESE COMMUTERS?

The majority of the new commuters were clerks – white-collar workers with incomes ranging from £150 (the threshold of income tax) to £700 pa. They now also included a growing number of local government and utility (gas, water, etc) employees and successful tradesmen, as well as professionals.

SALUBRIOUS SURROUNDINGS

Lower land values allowed larger plots of land for each house. This in turn allowed more light and air, which new legislation was trying to encourage – ineffectually at first. Moving out of town to the suburbs was regarded as highly desirable. Height above sea level and good drainage were the initial selling criteria, but the quality of an area reflected how carefully it had been developed.

Health consciousness was apparent in the changing design of the houses. Semi-detached houses began to appear and basements slowly decreased in numbers. The reputations of both terrace and basement were beginning to suffer. The service rooms could now be located elsewhere and builders could economise – cellars were cheaper to construct than basements.

Cellars were not intended for habitation but were used for storage of items such as coal. They allowed air to circulate under the house, which significantly reduced damp problems.

MEDIUM – *plan*

CHANGES IN PLAN

Another consequence of suburbanisation was the development of the rear extension. More space was available away from the city centres where land values were lower. The plots became deeper if not wider.

A rear extension or 'wing' began to fulfill the function of the basement, particularly if access from the rear of the plot was possible. The rear extension reduced the amount of work to be done – fewer floors to clean and less carrying up and down stairs.

HIERARCHY MAINTAINED

'Front' retained its superiority to 'back'. The rear extension was definitely 'back'. The face bricks for the side and back were usually inferior to those used for the front. The height of the rooms was only two thirds that of rooms in the main body of the house. It was a step down into the kitchen, both literally and socially. First-floor rooms branched off the half-landing, splitting the levels of back and front.

A MORE HYGIENIC HOME

Except for London, where land values remained high, the new plan allowed builders to dispense with the basement. This meant a very considerable saving. A two-storey, six-room house cost only £200 to build, as opposed to £345 with a basement.

Instead, they constructed a simple cellar. Cellars had other advantages besides being cheaper to build: there was ample space for the coal (one ton occupied about 45 cubic feet) and there was also proper ventilation, which greatly reduced damp and rot.

Last, but not least, the cellar conformed with contemporary ideas of a more hygienic home. The 'dark and malodorous' basement was no longer seen as desirable.

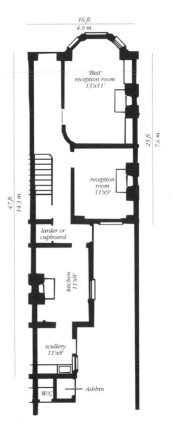

Above: Before the 1875 Public Health act. Ground floor – double lean-to extension. Small room opposite door to yard was sometimes used as a WC. Below: First floor – closet room in rear extension, other room was a bedroom.

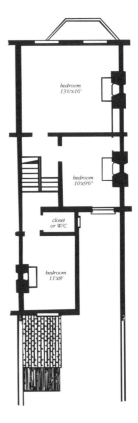

Cross-section: Note lower ceiling heights of rooms in rear extension. The combination of half-landing and steps down to rear extension creates a lower level.

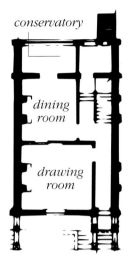

conservatory

Half-basement type: ground floor.

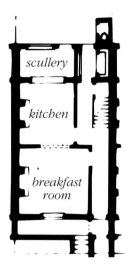

scullery

kitchen

breakfast room

Half-basement type: basement.

bedroom

bedroom

Half-basement type: first floor.

bedroom

bedroom

Half-basement type: second floor.

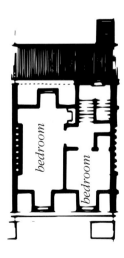

bedroom

bedroom

Half-basement type: attic floor.

Fireplace draperies.

STATUS AND ONE-UPMANSHIP

The suburbs ensured the separation of workplace from dwelling. Large residential areas consisting entirely of houses of the same class encouraged the practice of one-upmanship. Jealous of their status, the occupants strove either to prove their superiority to their middle-class neighbours or simply to 'keep up appearances'.

They concentrated on external details. A brief glimpse through the bay window or an impression gained from the hall might be all the visitor was allowed. Outside, the street was lined with lime, laburnum or acacia – smaller than the trees in the wider avenues of lofty mansions. Inside, 'opulence and comfort' more often meant clutter or slightly drawn curtains, revealing only an aspidistra plant, intended to conceal the bareness behind.

FIRST IMPRESSIONS

The hallway was the first, and sometimes only, part of the house that visitors would see. From there they would receive an impression of the social position of the residents. It was of prime importance to make a good first impression. The hallway also represented a conduit between the dark, cold outside world and the warmth and security of the home within.

Hallways were usually long and narrow, with little room for furniture, apart from a wooden coat and hat stand and a few chairs for visitors. This was made up for by elaborate decor. Many aspired to make it look like a hall in a country house and hung up stuffed heads, antlers and used heraldic glass in the door.

The hallways usually had a masculine flavour and strong, rich colours were a common choice. Light would be deflected through the stained-glass front door.

DRAPES AND DARK FINISHES

The heavy drapes were intended to keep out the harsh world outside. There were other reasons for the dark interior. The drapes, so strongly recommended by arbiters of taste in books and journals, were an insurance against direct light fading either precious hardwoods, 'grained' finishes or wallpapers. Faded finishes were 'down at heel'.

There was yet another reason for the dark colours – the dirt didn't show up so badly. In addition to the soot from their coal fires, their newly acquired gas lamps guttered over walls and ceilings. Also, when the lamps were lit, they gave out only pools of pale light rather than a wall-to-wall effect.

Fireplace draperies

MEDIUM – *back*

INFINITE VARIATIONS

There were infinite variations possible in the rear elevation. The basic pattern allowed windows to the rear-facing rooms in the main body of the house and to lower floors in the extension itself. A lean-to extension often accommodated the toilet and either scullery or ashbin.

BEFORE THE 1875 PUBLIC HEALTH ACT

Provision of sewers greatly improved following the 1848 Act, but until 1875 there was little effective regulation of toilets, cess and ash. The WC was still crude and smelly.

The backflow of gases from the sewer was not only noxious but also potentially explosive. Access to the toilet was usually from the outside. Some houses avoided windows overlooking the toilet. Houses of a similar type built later (when plumbing had improved further) had a window in the rear-end wall.

ASHBIN

The other vital amenity was the ash or dustbin for the residue of the coal fires. This was the principal cause of all rubbish. The average house produced three loads each year, amounting to as much as eleven tons. The local parish was now responsible for collection.

COUPLED REAR EXTENSIONS

There was considerable development of the rear extension. This development had begun as builders realised the benefits that were to be gained by coupling the rear extensions of neighbouring houses – more head room in the rear extension and the warmth of a party wall, not to mention the saving in building costs.

Later, they realised the rear wing could actually accommodate more floors than the main body due to the lower floors and ceilings and the flatter pitch of the roof.

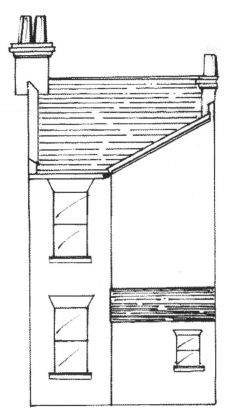

Entrance to WC is from left-hand side. Window on right is over sink in scullery. Ashbin is situated elsewhere

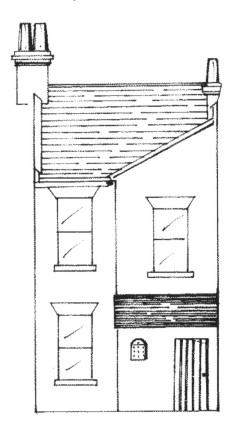

Door in lean-to extension is for the ashbin. Toilet now has small ventilation grill. Window above is evidence of better plumbing. Windows levels are lower than in main body

Estate plan – note coupled rear extensions, houses all of a similar size and the nearby suburban railway lines.

Above: Rear elevation of half-basement type; the rear extension stretches the full width of the house at basement and ground-floor levels. The ashbin had its own out-house (left). There were two rear exits, from the corridor and the scullery respectively.

A lower middle-class family gardening.

Cold Water	Hot Water	Kitchen Range	WC	Gas
yes	1869 onwards	yes	yes	yes

MIDDLE-CLASS INSECURITY

The insecurity of the middle classes expressed itself in their concern for 'correct' taste and hierarchy within the home. With regard to taste, they preferred to adopt the hard and fast rules of other 'authorities' on decor; a plethora of manuals were being produced to meet this demand, the most famous being Mrs Beeton's *Book of Household Management*.

Fireplaces were an immediate guide to the importance of a room. Marble was 'best', followed by slate. In the bedrooms they were smaller, possibly made from cast iron and painted. If the servant's room had one, it would be smaller still, with a painted wooden surround.

COME INTO THE GARDEN, MAUD!

The music-hall song echoes the aspirations of the occupants of the first middle-class suburbs. They had real gardens rather than utilitarian yards. The garden of the medium-sized house was planned to be a microcosm of that of the larger. Conservatory, exotic plants and lawns were intended to create an idyllic retreat.

Only in one respect did the middle class fail to follow their social superiors: they would not grow vegetables. They did not need to because the growing railway network ensured ample supplies in the new shops which were developing to cater for them. But there was also the powerful need to differentiate themselves from the working class who might grow their own supplies.

MOWING THE LAWN

Instead, they concentrated on their lawns and flowers. The lawnmower, first invented in 1830, was advertised with a smartly-dressed 'gentleman' in control. Gardening was therefore socially acceptable for both middle-class men and women.

However, the area just at the back of the house was still utilitarian. Unless the garden was deep enough, the 'pastoral retreat' might be spoilt by the unpleasant odour of crude and inefficient drains, an open ashpit or piles of rubbish.

An arrangement for the conservatory.

SMALL – *front*

PERIOD OF IMPROVEMENT

There were three reasons for improvements in the building of workers' housing:

1. National legislation.

2. A substantial rise in workers' wages.

3. The Model Housing Movement.

NATIONAL LEGISLATION

Acts of Parliament provided mechanisms of control for sanitation, health and building standards. These had to be enforced locally through 'bylaws'. The most important piece of legislation was the 1848 Health Act, which was intended to improve sanitation and services.

RISE IN WAGES

It has been estimated that workers' wages rose by thirty per cent between 1850 and 1875. This was perhaps the main reason for the improvement in their housing – they could afford better homes.

THE MODEL HOUSING MOVEMENT

This movement provided the ideas upon which the legislation was based.

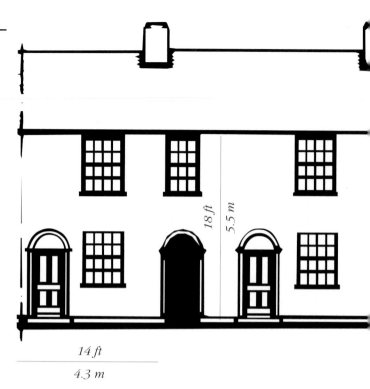

18 ft
5.5 m

14 ft
4.3 m

Back-to-back houses continued to be built for the working classes in large numbers, particularly in the North, North-West, North-East and Midlands. The central doorway led directly to the yard or court.

A well laid out estate designed for working-class families. This sort of development required a considerable amount of philanthropic involvement.

Through house in the South-East, built as a semi-detached pair with rear access at the side. This type of house was often shared by more than one family.

A well-publicised model-house design which drew attention to the need for better housing for the working classes.

Designs like these were too expensive for the speculative builders to use, but began to influence health and building regulations.

RISE IN WAGES

After the middle of the nineteenth century, conditions for the working classes began to improve. Social concern began to grow at the same time as the likelihood of political upheaval diminished. But without a rise in their wages, the working class wouldn't have been able to afford better accommodation. In fact, their wages did increase as the overall wealth of the country grew.

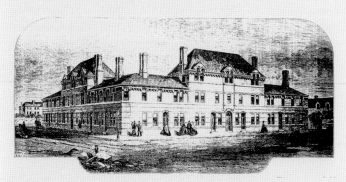

A model housing design 'for the Labouring classes'. Designs such as this one and that shown in the left-hand column chiefly influenced the design of tenements, or flats. Whatever the outcome of such designs, the vast proportion of the urban working class were housed by spec builders.

MODEL HOUSING MOVEMENT

Some of the new industrialists were moved to build 'model' housing estates for the workers in their factories. Partly philanthropic, partly pragmatic, the gesture assured them of a healthy, loyal workforce.

Model housing estates such as the famous ones at Saltaire and Akroyden consisted of well laid out houses and such amenities as a school, church and an institute with a library, lecture room and reading room.

The houses themselves were built to a high standard: the kitchens had sinks with piped water, boilers and ovens by their fireplaces. Outside, each had a private backyard with a privy. Some of the houses had a living-room as well as a back kitchen and three bedrooms above.

Rents were low and the developers received only a five per cent return on their investment rather than the normal ten to eleven per cent. A typical weekly rent was 1s 6d – 6d more than the other houses, but as families brought home anything from 24s to 50s a week it was still affordable.

The attitude of the owners was paternalistic – at Saltaire there were restrictions on alcohol and the motto of the Ashworth's was 'Thrift, Order, Promptitude and Reverence'. It was unfortunate that model housing formed only a very small percentage of the housing built for the working class.

SMALL – *plan*

BIGGER HOUSES
Houses became bigger again. The average size of a through-house plot was 15ft wide by 36ft deep. They were now built to a higher standard, but still lacked a hallway. The stairs, however, were sometimes brought towards the front.

LIVING-ROOMS OR PARLOUR?
The model-housing movement insisted that the houses should have two living-rooms, but the workers would have liked a parlour. Specifically, they wanted a room that could be kept for special occasions. Without a hall, the second living-room was just another communal living space.

New houses were built with a cellar which provided important cool storage space.

SEPARATE BEDROOMS FOR BOYS AND GIRLS
Housing reformers were beginning to advocate separate bedrooms for boys and girls – previously a privilege of the servant-keeping classes – consequently houses now required at least two or three bedrooms.

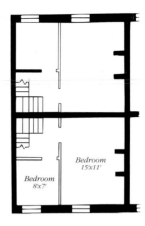

First floors of a pair of back-to-backs.

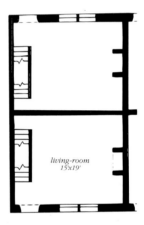

Ground floor of a pair of back-to-backs.

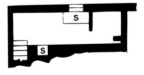

Basement of a pair of back-to-backs.

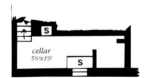

The house-place (main living-room) of a working-class home in 1872.

In London, where there were relatively few back-to-backs, workers would share a medium-sized house with another family.

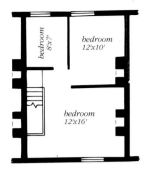

Ground floor   First floor

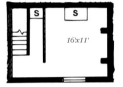

Basement

Small through house with stairs placed at the front. Typical occupants would have been a colliery foreman and his family.

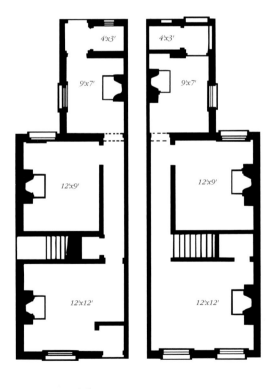

Ground floor   First floor

An unusually spacious, small through house with entrance lobby, centrally-placed staircases and rear extension. It is likely to have been shared by more than one family.

PERMANENT BUILDING SOCIETIES

Prior to 1842, building clubs were 'terminating': once their members were all housed, they ceased to exist. After an Act of Parliament in 1842, they were allowed to become 'permanent building societies', which continued to function after their original members had all been housed. Permanent building societies had the advantage of retaining the expertise acquired in housing their original members and keeping intact pools of capital which were essential to the building process.

Permanent building societies also had an additional goal of enabling their members to vote by meeting the property qualification – a freehold with a rateable value of 40s per annum.

Permanent building societies were very successful and their commercial role became their real function. They lent money to all categories of builders and original borrowers included millhands, ironworkers, labourers and domestic servants.

The greatest difficulty for lower-paid house buyers was to qualify for a loan by putting down an initial deposit, usually about a quarter of the cost of the property. Some building societies, like the Halifax, required no deposit and others had schemes where it could be repaid over a period of twenty years.

Speculative builders could borrow money on an 'advance and suspension policy', where they needed only to make payments to cover the interest while building was going on; the lump sum was repaid when the property was sold.

Like the model-housing movement, the permanent building societies played an important role in setting standards. To safeguard their investment, they ensured that properties met minimum requirements.

HOUSE DEVELOPMENTS

Fitted cupboards were built in the recesses next to the chimney breast, and in the cellars, scullery and pantry, shelves were made of stone.

Most working-class townspeople took their food, especially their bread and dinners, to the 'bake house' to be cooked. There was usually a bake house conveniently close and they were often located in the cellars of corner shops. The bake houses were popular for two reasons: first, the cooking facilities in the houses were still minimal, often consisting of only a hotplate or two, and secondly, working wives had little time for cooking.

SMALL – *back*

BENEFITS ACROSS THE BOARD

The back-to-backs benefited similarly, becoming larger, with the first floor divided into two or even three rooms.

Rents for the new houses were higher due to the increased building costs of the better accommodation, but many workers could afford to pay more as wages were actually rising faster than rents. A new back-to-back was 1s 6d a week in 1860. Rents for better accommodation could be as much as 6s a week.

REAL IMPROVEMENT

The 1848 Health Act had a great influence on the backs. The most important effect of the legislation was to ensure access to the back so that cess, ash and rubbish could be removed.

The standard now was for each dwelling to have a privy allocated to it. The yards became bigger to make this possible.

Back-to-backs might still have shared ashbins, and access to the rear was probably through a lobby – this was a narrow tunnel which had to be at least six feet wide. Narrow walls were built between yards.

The backs were still cramped, but it was a real improvement.

Cold Water	Hot Water	Kitchen Range	WC	Gas
possibly	no	no	no	no

Below: The backs of small houses in London in 1870, dominated by railway arches and suburban railway lines. The small rear extensions have chimney flues for set-pots, hence the nearby water butt. The rear-access lane was very narrow, as was usual in the mid-Victorian period 1850–75.

Sketch of a yard showing the tunnel flanked by the doors of the houses into the yard. In the foreground are outhouses for privies, ash and rubbish.

Left: Further evidence of improvement: grass plots in front of some of the houses.

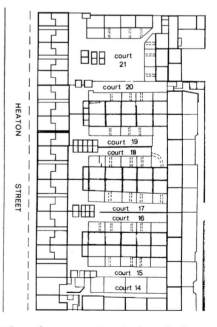

Plan of courts in Birmingham built after the 1848 Public Health Act.

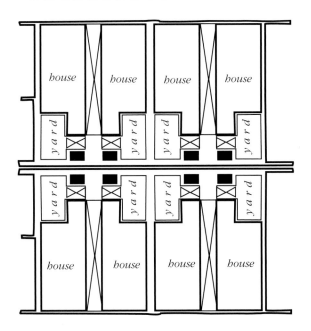

street

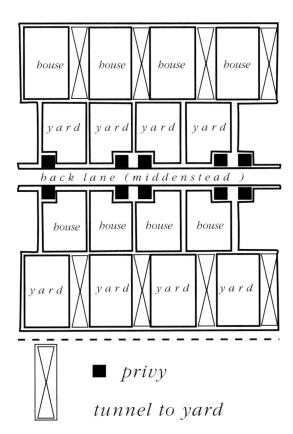

street

back lane (middenstead)

■ privy

☒ tunnel to yard

After the 1848 Public Health act: tunnel access to the back yards.

BETTER BACKS

The Public Health Act of 1848 laid down guidelines for the local authorities to interpret and enforce through 'bylaws'. The net result was improved access to the backs for rubbish and ash collection.

The health problem continued to be serious until proper sewers were built to service working-class areas. The latest areas to be developed for them had better street layout which enabled drains and sewers to be laid. Local people with vested interests could still thwart such schemes if they were both determined and sufficiently well-placed to do so.

WHO GOT THE THROUGHS?

To benefit from such improvements meant, of course, moving into newly-built accommodation, hence the importance of the wage rises. Foremen and skilled workers were best placed to take advantage of this. It was these 'Non-Comissioned Officers of the Working Classes' who got the through houses. The latter were available in greater numbers than before, although they were not yet the majority of small houses being built.

More space and light meant less illness, and better disposal of rubbish, ash and cess.

BANNING LIVESTOCK

In 1848 the Public Health Act forbade the keeping of livestock in backyards. Unfortunately, it took time before there were any bylaws to make the Act enforceable.

WATER SUPPLIES

The people behind the Public Health Act pressed continually to improve the sanitary conditions in workers' houses. Their primary aim was to replace the privies, but it was a long process. First, sewer pipes had to be installed to remove the effluent, but the laying of drains could not keep up with the rapid increase in population. Secondly, water had to be pumped in and this led to the final problem: many cities had an insufficient supply of water to feed all the houses. In many cases, there was barely enough for the taps, let alone a water closet.

Above left: A privy arrangement – the pail was removed through the door. Above right: A privy pail.

EPILOGUE

Arbiters of taste.

LARGE

The concept of 'taste' was still prevalent, but there was a choice of different forms. The Victorian interpretation of the classical was now only one of a variety from which to choose. Contemporaries were still inclined to insist on the propriety of their own particular choice.

MEDIUM

Once again, the form of the mediums followed that of the large. It, too, showed some variation in plan – the long terraces were beginning to be interrupted by semi-detached houses, which were somewhat pretentiously called 'villas'.

Middle-class pretensions – and clutter.

Basements were no longer standard: their reputation had suffered too much from the bad press given to insanitary cellar dwellings. Anyway, they were no longer absolutely necessary in the more spacious suburbs, where lower land values allowed medium houses to be built on larger plots. These larger plots were able to accommodate the services in a sizeable rear extension.

The new suburbs had been made possible by the development of suburban railways and horse buses. The population of these suburbs was exclusively middle class – the first time any class had lived entirely apart from any other.

Better housing was within the means of the working class.

SMALL

Overall, the new small houses were a distinct improvement. Social concern had led to legislation which, although not universally effective, resulted in better dwellings for those who could afford them. The vital fact was that many could.

LATE VICTORIAN 1876-99

The last quarter of the nineteenth century saw a number of different cultural movements, including the Arts and Crafts Movement, the Aesthetic Movement and numerous retrospective forms. Prominent among the up-to-date building forms was that of the Queen Anne Revival.

STATE OF THE NATION

Britain's international position began to change. Other nations were catching up economically, which began to cause cycles at home of booms and slumps. Cheap imports of grain led to a decline in the influence of the landed class and henceforward wealth would come from finance rather than land. Consequently, the balance of power shifted towards the middle classes, who became much more assertive – both politically and culturally.

The country's wealth, however, was still increasing. This was expressed in buying power rather than wage rises. Essential goods were less expensive due to competition from foreign imports.

CULTURE VULTURES

Many members of the new generation rejected the notion that one artistic form was morally superior to another. Instead, these people were more concerned with individuality and beauty. The beautiful, they

Those who prized individuality and beauty were caricatured as passionate aesthetes. In this satirical scene, a couple are admiring a teapot. Aesthetic Bridegroom: *'It is exquisite, is it not?'* Intense Bride: *'It is indeed! Oh, Algernon, let us live up to it!'*.

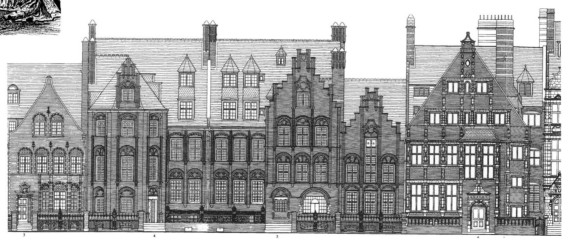

The Queen Anne Revival placed a strong emphasis on individuality. Each house varied as much as possible from its neighbours, even in a terrace.

perceived, was something that could be found in many different forms. Their emphasis on individuality epitomised both their reaction to mass production and their own middle-class origins.

THE STYLE

The Queen Anne Revival style was architect led, but these men knew and worked with the leaders of the Arts and Crafts Movement and the Aesthetic Movement. Both movements had a strong influence on the spirit and practical design of houses during this period.

THE ARTS AND CRAFTS MOVEMENT

Led by William Morris, the Arts and Crafts Movement advocated a return to the individually-crafted artefacts of the past. In fact, eschewing modern production techniques made the products too expensive for any but the well-to-do.

AESTHETIC MOVEMENT

The Aesthetic Movement was more a way of thinking than a design movement. The Aesthetics were keen to shed the values of the previous generation, which they regarded as stultifying. Instead, they replaced them with an opening of the

Numerous architects were following the revivalist path: an illustration from the frontispiece of Richardson's Picturesque Designs for Mansions *(1870).*

Gothic continued in popularity, but the periods from which the forms were taken changed. By the 1870s, architects were producing designs known as Tudorbethan – combining Tudor and Elizabethan elements.

Dutch and Flemish architecture was an acknowledged influence on the Queen Anne Revival.

mind to 'sweetness and light' – in other words, to the possibilities of beauty and relevance in all things according to individual perception. To the older or more orthodox Victorians, it seemed a rather nebulous, 'artistic' philosophy.

QUEEN ANNE DESIGN

The architects hired by the newly-assertive middle classes delved into the styles of the past. They came up with numerous revivalist forms, including Elizabethan, Jacobean and Queen Anne.

It was the Queen Anne that became the predominant form of this 'Domestic Revival', because it could be either extravagant or economical. The speculative builders found it easy to copy and many of the lower middle classes adored it.

Those who criticised the new movements chose to live in houses that continued in the classical design.

An example of the original Queen Anne style, which combined classical and vernacular forms in warm red brick.

Warm red brick at Bedford Park, the archetypal Queen Anne Revival estate.

LARGE – *front*

RED BRICK STYLE

The most immediately noticeable feature of the new style was the use of colour; the predominant feature was red brick, often accompanied by horizontal white banding.

Windows changed in style, size and shape. Casements were reintroduced and the emphasis of the overall proportions altered as the top third of the window received most attention.

Pediments were used over doors, windows and gables, continuing the vertical feel of the preceding Italian and Gothic forms. First straight, Dutch gables then curved, Flemish gables began to be used in the designs.

Design was carried to the roof line. Chimneys became a prominent feature in their own right and often dominated the building they served. The taller, the better was the thinking.

OTHER KEY IDENTIFIABLE STYLE FEATURES

These included moulded brickwork, terracotta, pargeting, hooded doorcases, oriel windows, quoining, overhanging eaves and ridge decoration – all from vernacular architecture, hence the expression Domestic Revival.

The lower land values of the suburbs allowed semi-detached and villa houses to be built in greater numbers than ever before. The red-brick Queen Anne style was adopted by architects and speculative builders alike.

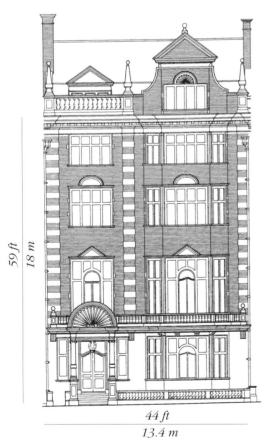

59 ft
18 m

44 ft
13.4 m

Only where land values were still at a premium, as in London, did the large terraced house continue to be built. However, these large terraced houses provided some of the finest examples of the Queen Anne Revival.

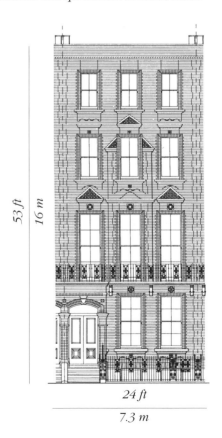

53 ft
16 m

24 ft
7.3 m

Variation was part and parcel of the Queen Anne Revival. This example avoided the usual white horizontal banding and instead relied on moulded red-brick decoration.

Dutch and Flemish gables were incorporated in the design of houses in Cadogan Gardens to create a profusion of form in which every house was different.

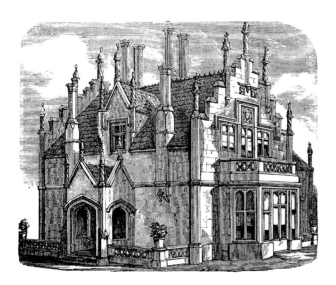

A Tudorbethan style semi-detached villa.

THE THIRD GENERATION

The Victorians who bought or lived in the new style were well educated, sophisticated and cultured. They were more confident about expressing their own taste and less in awe of the upper class. Not only did they have money, but they were now more powerful and had influence of their own.

THE IDYLLIC PAST

Many who were active in the Arts and Crafts Movement believed that society in the past had been better, both materially and morally. There was a new love for the features of modest buildings which created a 'vernacular or domestic revival'. They no longer wanted houses that looked like palaces, but ones that looked like cottages.

The supposed working-class values of thrift and simplicity were adopted, together with the simple but solid style of their houses. Old-fashioned materials were employed and the new houses were built of brickwork, had steeply-pitched roofs, were hung with plain tiles and had small casement windows. The ideal house was smallish-looking and hidden behind greenery.

MOTIFS OF THE MOVEMENT

Various symbols became associated with the new movement, the most prevalent being the sunflower. It was used extensively by Morris, Rossetti and Burne-Jones, who had adopted it from their favourite poets – Blake and Tennyson.

Sunflower motif in ironwork.

Originally, they seemed to use it as a symbol of physical love and the world of the senses. On a more prosaic level, from the 1860s onwards the sunflower, both potted and unpotted, appeared on houses in terracotta panels. These were set into the external walls under the eaves or between the doors and windows. The front gardens at Bedford Park, the original Aesthetic estate, were even planted with sunflowers.

Other popular motifs were the lily and the peacock, which featured largely in the products sold at the new Liberty store.

Simple but solid style: a dresser.

LARGE − *plan*

TERRACE

The terrace form was fairly conventional, but the back of the house continued to grow in importance because of its proximity to the garden. Major rooms like the dining-room or study were now placed there.

The drawing-room was still on the first floor. New recreational rooms – the billiard room, smoking-room, etc – were located either on the first floor or the ground floor.

For the first time, bathrooms were included in the original design of the house and were usually situated on the second floor. Water closets also appeared on the upper floors as a consequence of the improvements in water services – higher pressure, increased availability and more sophisticated new plumbing.

More bedrooms were added, especially for servants. Senior servants, the butler and the housekeeper usually had rooms in the basement close to the kitchen and wine cellar. The basement itself was now full of rooms designated for particular use, such as the pantry, wine-cellar and scullery.

VILLA

The villa differed in that the major reception rooms were all on the ground floor and the connection with the garden was easily achieved over the half-basement by terracing and steps.

A wider plot meant that all the rooms considered essential could be fitted in without building above the second (attic) floor.

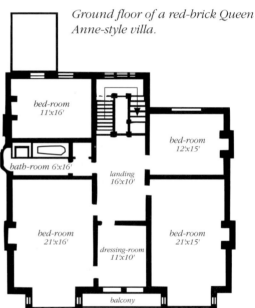

Ground floor of a red-brick Queen Anne-style villa.

First floor of a red-brick Queen Anne-style villa.

A stylish interior of the 1880s.

Side view of a Tudorbethan-type villa, showing steps down into the garden (right).

Terrace: basement.

Terrace: ground floor.

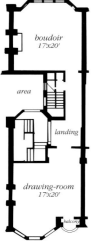

Terrace: first floor.

Terrace: second floor.

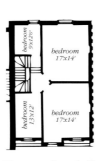

Terrace: third floor.

Terrace: fourth floor.

HYGIENIC BATHROOMS

Concern for health led to bathrooms becoming more hygienic. They began to be purpose built and were smaller and more streamlined. The floors and walls up to the dado were covered with ceramic tiles. Pipes and sanitary fittings were left exposed, making them easier to clean to counteract hidden germs.

Bathtubs with ball or claw feet were now free standing so that they could be washed underneath. Needle and spray showers were commercially available and fitted in the bath. 'Lavatories' or washbasins also had their plumbing on view. They were suspended from ornamental iron brackets or supported on metal legs.

Decoration moved from the room itself to the fittings, which were painted or stencilled with matching floral patterns. The exposed pipes, made from brass or copper, gleamed from regular polishing and were an additional attractive feature.

By the end of the century, fashion was changing and plain, white, neo-classical bathroom fittings with brass, nickel or porcelain taps became the most popular.

Advertisement for the new incandescent lights.

BRIGHT LIGHT

When the Austrian Baron Auer von Welsbach invented the incandescent mantel in 1884, he brought light to Victorian evenings. The mantel produced twice the amount of light as the existing jet burners without increasing the consumption of gas. The incandescent mantel glowed white hot when heated by the burning gas.

At about the same time, the electric light bulb also appeared. It operated on a similar principle of heating an element inside a glass envelope until it, too, shone white hot.

Unfortunately, the development of electric lighting by private enterprise was discouraged for several years until the Electrical Lighting Act of 1888 was passed.

The brighter light transformed life in many ways – suddenly revealing to the inhabitants how over-furnished their rooms looked and how crude colour schemes were.

89

LARGE – *back*

TERRACE

The garden at the rear was taking over in importance from the prospect – square or crescent – in front. So much so that the large houses shared one communal back garden between them as they had done the square in front.

The layout of these gardens remained relatively formal because they were shared. The individual houses had access to them over rear-facing terraces, which were built over the basement service rooms.

VILLA

Villas stood in their own gardens and offered access to them from as many rooms in the house as possible. French doors opened on to steps leading down to a path or lawn.

IMPROVEMENT IN SERVICES

Drains, plumbing and refuse disposal had all improved so much that they were now able to say 'out of sight was out of mind'.

Garden front of a Gothic villa.

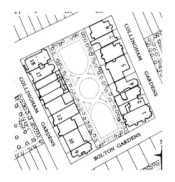

Estate plan of terraced houses showing orientation towards the shared gardens at the back.

Late nineteenth-century garden plan: overgrown, naturalistic look.

Interior of a drawing-room showing the orientation towards the garden.

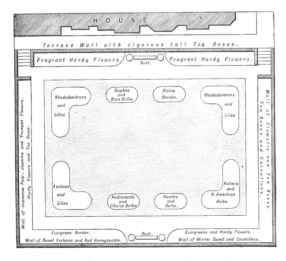

Late nineteenth-century garden plan: wide lawn with herbaceous borders.

In suburban gardens, the new game of lawn tennis was possible. Ladies could also participate.

The 'natural', overgrown approach to the back of the house and the garden, as advocated by William Robinson.

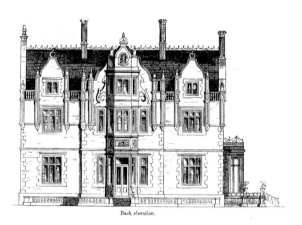

Back elevation.

Rear elevation of a Tudorbethan villa showing balcony and steps to the garden.

Steps to the garden, balustrade and garden gate.

Cold Water	Hot Water	Kitchen Range	WC	Gas
yes	yes	yes	yes	yes

COMMUNAL GARDENS

Until now, the backs of the large terraced houses were usually uncared for. Backs meant service and the members of the family would never venture there. However, the backs of the newly-designed terraces – for example, those on the Ladbroke Estate in North Kensington – faced directly on to communal gardens. Not even separated by a road, the garden was accessible from the living-room which was still on the first floor.

This meant that the service parts were squeezed back into the basement, but they spilled out into the rear. They were bridged and disguised by balustraded terraces with steps into the garden. These houses were expensive as they needed facades both at the front and the back.

THE NATURAL GARDEN

The Arts and Crafts Movement, inspired by the traditional country cottage garden, created the return of the 'natural' garden.

The most important gardening writer at the time – William Robinson – said that the garden 'should rise out of its site and conditions as happily as a primrose out of a cool bank'.

Formal layout and bedding plants were eschewed. Instead, wide lawns, herbaceous borders and informal groups of wild flowers became the ideal, with rustic winding paths of gravel or grass.

Old-fashioned flowers were sought out – sunflowers, hollyhocks, lilies and poppies were much used – as well as the old standard roses, chosen more for what they represented than the flowers themselves.

Garden furniture became simpler, with plain benches made of oak or elm. Terracotta flowerpots, low stone troughs and sundials were the only garden ornaments.

Simple form of garden seat.

Simple oak pale fence.

MEDIUM – *front*

SQUARE BAYS AND RED BRICK

Medium quickly followed the fashion set by large. Red brick was the easiest feature to emulate, followed by white horizontal banding.

Not all bays were canted – some were now square. These square bays were shallower and broader, and actually brought more light into the rooms. Sometimes the builders alternated canted and square bays along a terrace.

Because of the bay, the doorway appeared to be recessed. Doorways received their own small roofs, sometimes edged with fretwork.

Casement windows were expensive, but builders achieved a similar effect by using the standard sash and placing all the leading in the top part.

Triangular gables and dormers were popular.

MAJOR CHANGE

There was neither a basement nor railings. A service entrance was provided to one side.

Below right: A double front showing two houses with as much variation between them as was possible for medium houses. The right-hand house has a separate servants' entrance (far right).

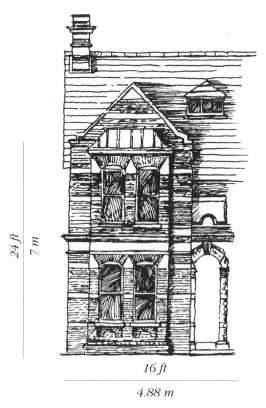

24 ft
7 m

16 ft

4.88 m

Red brick was the most common feature of the Queen Anne Revival style, frequently accompanied by white horizontal banding. Many bay windows were square rather than angled and gables increased the vertical emphasis.

25 ft

7.6 m

24.6 ft

7.3 m

24 ft
7 m

16 ft
4.88 m

Builders often mixed and matched different forms and features. The two-storey bay has half-hips, which gave it a vertical, kind of Gothic feel, while the mouldings on lintels and door arches were vaguely classical. Houses of this design were often built with the red facing brick made fashionable by the Queen Anne Revival. Many others were built in grey or yellow brick, giving them either a more classical or a more Gothic look.

Half-timbered treatment, especially on the gables, with roughcast finish on the upper floors constituted the Old English look. This was originally intended to be the rural counterpart of the urban Queen Anne form. However, towards the end of the nineteenth century the speculative builders began to use it more and more in the new suburbs.

'MIDDLE' MIDDLE CLASS

One way of defining the middle class was by income. Middle-class incomes began at £150, the income tax threshold, and continued up to £700.

By the 1890s, they had grown to over thirteen per cent of the total population. The class continued to expand. Clerical duties were dividing into three categories: management, technical and sales.

Many looked up not to the very rich upper class, but to the well-off upper middle class. It was their new smart style these aspirants wanted to copy.

They contributed to a growing public interest in art, which they wished to display in their homes. If they lacked confidence in their own taste, there was a growing number of monthly magazines to advise them.

LIBERTY & CO

Liberty & Co was established by Arthur Lasenby Liberty in 1875. It produced and distributed clothes, fabric, metalwork and furniture to a much larger section of the public than that catered to by William Morris's company. Liberty & Co used manufacturers who could produce goods mechanically at a fraction of the cost of their competitors. One of the aims of the store was to refine public taste and aesthetic standards in England.

Interior of one of the new Department Stores, similar to Liberty, which catered for the growing middle class.

SPECULATIVE BUILDERS

Speculative builders for the middle-income bracket jumped on the 'vernacular' or 'domestic' revival style as quickly as they had on all previous ones that had been inaugurated by the architects.

Building News in 1895 estimated that a builder could run up a house fifty per cent less expensively than an architect. The new notion of the 'ideal' family dwelling was taken up by the speculative builders and they, too, built smaller versions of the Queen Anne style.

MEDIUM – *plan*

BROADER PLOTS

Plots were often broader and more rooms could be brought into the main body of the house, including the kitchen – although this was still set at a slightly lower floor level.

The rear main reception room connected directly with the garden via a conservatory or French doors.

This new house plan was less labour intensive.

UPSTAIRS

The new features upstairs were the bathroom and the WC.

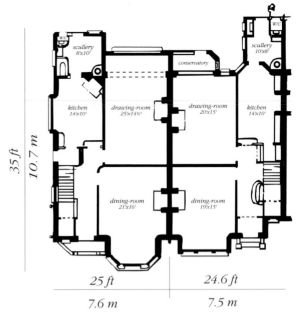

Pair of houses: ground floor.

Interior of a typical reception room in the 1890s. Carpet and rugs on the floor, doorway drapes, valance over the mantelpiece, sideboard and crudely-hung pictures.

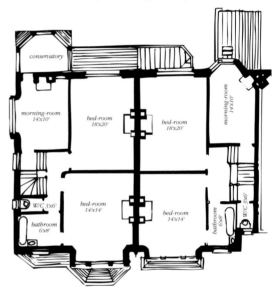

Pair of houses: first floor.

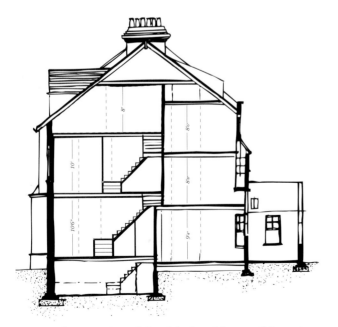

Cross-section of the right hand house of the pair.

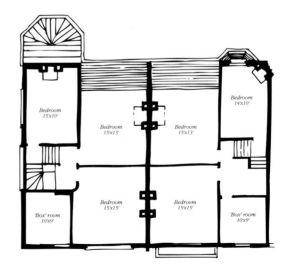

Pair of houses: second floor.

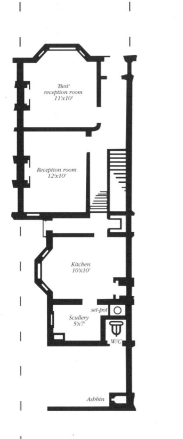

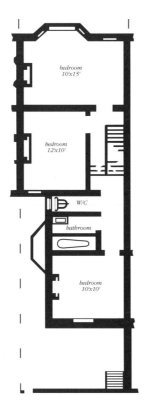

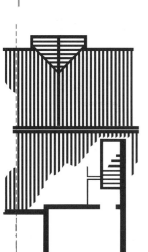

After the 1875 Public Health act: split-level type (above) ground and first floors. Scullery now in main part of rear 'wing'. WC and bathroom are upstairs.

Below left: Second floor in rear 'wing'.

Above right: Houseplants in the hall.

WALLPAPERS

It was William Morris who had the most dramatic influence on wallpaper design. He rejected the three-dimensional scenes that had been popular and created flat, rhythmical patterns based both on medieval motifs and on nature. These were handpainted by his company Morris and Co and copied by the mass producers.

His first papers 'Daisy', 'Fruit' and 'Trellis', were inspired by the flowers and fruit found in his garden at the Red House. A large range of papers were subsequently produced in warm, subtle colours using traditional vegetable dyes. The most popular colours were rust, sage green and peacock blue and gold.

Some of the patterns were inspired by Renaissance tapestries and used by those who could not afford the real thing. Most of the houses in Bedford Park had wallpapers in the design of William Morris and they are still available today.

ENCAUSTIC TILES

The use of tiles for domestic floors revived when Herbert Minton developed the encaustic tile in 1840. This method involved the inlaying of different coloured clays and fusing them together during firing.

Numerous factories sprung up in response to the demand for the tiles, which became a highly popular decorative item both inside and outside the house on floors and walls. That arbiter of late Victorian taste Charles Eastlake gave them his hearty approval: 'for beauty of effect, durability, and cheapness...scarcely a parallel'.

The tiles were produced in a variety of styles, both pictorial and plain, in the natural colours of clay – white, black, red and cream. Later, they were also made with chemical dyes in green, blue and lilac. Designs were supplied by leading architects.

HIERARCHY OF LOO SEATS

Servants were usually not allowed to use the same water closet as their employers, but differences in status extended to the 'loos' themselves. Seats made of mahogany or walnut and polished to a high sheen were fitted to the water closet used by the family, while that used by the servants was constructed from inexpensive, untreated white pine and colloquially referred to as a 'scrubbable'. Scrubbed it was, too, on a regular basis by the lowest servant in the household.

MEDIUM – *back*

QUEEN ANNE FRONT, MARY ANNE BACK

For reasons of economy, the elegant features of the front were not continued around the sides and back; not even the red brick itself. The sides and backs of the medium houses were usually built from cheaper, local 'stock' brick. Hence the contemporary joke 'Queen Anne front, Mary Anne back'.

ENJOYABLE GARDENS

The middle classes also wanted to enjoy their gardens. Indeed, they were much pleasanter places once legislation had ensured that effective services were a necessary part of all house design. The problem of noxious gases from the main sewer was eliminated by the 'disconnecting trap'.

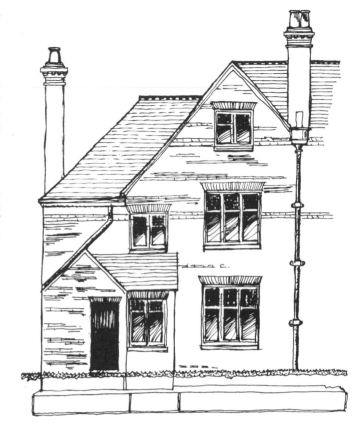

Rear elevation of the left-hand house of the pair shown on the previous pages.

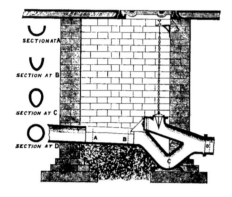

The vital improvement in drainage was the intercepting trap: a water-trap that prevented the smell from the main sewer getting into the house.

Cold Water	Hot Water	Kitchen Range	WC	Gas
yes	yes	yes	yes	yes

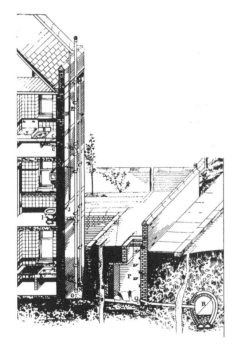

Cut-away view of the back showing how the improved drainage and sanitation worked.

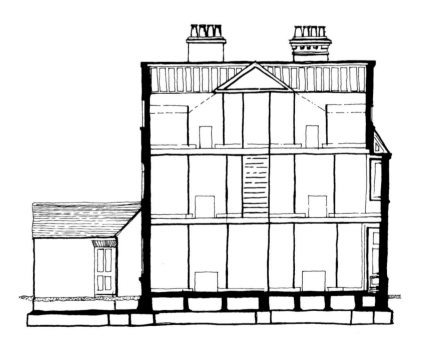

Cross-section of the left-hand house of the pair shown on the previous pages.

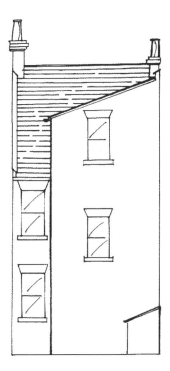

Rear elevation of split-level type, which accommodated a second floor in the rear extension.

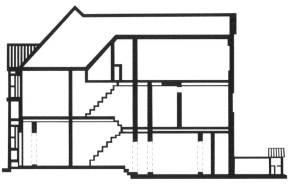

Cross-section of split-level type, which accommodated a second floor in the rear extension.

Garden path with stone edging to flower-beds.

OPENING THE BACK

The most important new tendency in house design was to open the house to the rear garden by placing the largest room, usually the dining-room, at the back of the extension.

French doors were used to give direct access to the garden itself. This often led to an even wider and bulkier back extension, leaving even less space for the windows at the back of the main part of the house. The kitchen and the breakfast-room were placed at the back and the breakfast-room was often given a bay window to give it more importance and for it to receive additional light.

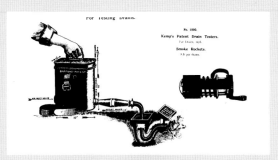

Equipment used in drain tests.

SMOKE AND PEPPERMINT TESTS

The drains gave offence on occasion. The offensive odour was usually due to leaks, which the plumbers were called in to locate. To do this, they would pump smoke down the toilet and wait for it to emerge through the floor showing where the trouble spot was.

The smoke drain testers could be extremely powerful and if the drains were really decrepit, the house became so full of smoke that it had to be evacuated until the air cleared.

This was obviously inconvenient and the peppermint test was invented as a substitute. Oil of peppermint was added to the water in the bowl of the WC and flushed through. Then the plumbers dashed about, sniffing out the peppermint odour around the house.

The ideal, as depicted by The Garden *magazine.*

THE SMELL OF HORSES

Everywhere outside smelt of horses as they were still the most common form of transportation. The small back gardens were manured with dung, which was shovelled up from the street and sold door to door.

SMALL – *front*

BYLAW BENEFITS

For the first time, the majority of small houses being built were through houses. Better-off artisans enjoyed the benefits of the new bylaws, which gave them not only better standards of construction, but more decorative features than the medium had had at the beginning of the century.

DETAILS

Proper lintels, brick arches over windows, decorative brick work, bargeboards on dormer windows, well-finished chimneys and roof ridges were now standard features of the small through house.

Speculatively-built through house.

Houses in Birmingham built by the Corporation. Publicly-funded building still formed only a tiny proportion of the small houses being built.

'Working men's flats' looked like medium-sized houses, but were actually designed as separate flats.

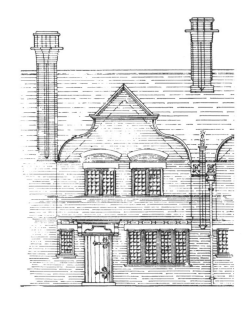

Houses in Port Sunlight, a model town built by Lever Bros for their employees; impressive but too elaborate for the speculative builders.

Speculatively-built through house with a bay window.

Late nineteenth-century back-to-back: although gradually being banned by local authorities because of their dubious reputation, they continued to be built.

WORKERS MOVE TO SUBURBIA

The working class had either toiled on the land and led a rural life or lived close to their place of work in the city centres. But the third generation of Victorian working class saw housing being built for them (as well as the middle class) in the suburbs.

The estates were developed on distinct sites so there was no mixing of the classes. Ne'er the twain should meet, even when travelling to and from their places of work. To ensure this, special 'workers trains' were laid on at five and six o'clock in the morning – before the professional commuters were up and about. Cheaper fares were introduced for the workers to enable them to be able to afford to commute. But the tram was more popular for the commuting working class. It was far cheaper than the train, twice as fast as a horse-bus and wasn't so much the territory of the middle class.

WORKING-CLASS WAGE CHART

Job	Weekly wages	Rent paid	Type of house
Foremen Skilled workers (Artisans)	40s	7s	Through
Semi-skilled workers	20s–35s	2s–3s	Shared or back-to-back
Unskilled workers Local utility workers (gas and water companies) Lowly council employees Female textile workers	14s–20s	1s–2s	Shared or back-to-back

£1 = 20s (shillings) = 100p (new pence). 1s = 12 old pence = 5p

Late nineteenth century: unrelieved rows of working-class housing.

SMALL – *plan*

VARIATIONS IN PLAN

There were variations in the ground plans. Non-hall and half-hall types predominated. The half-hall created the much sought after parlour, although it was still tiny.

A separate 'wash-house' or scullery was added. The law now dictated the provision of a WC or earth closet, ashbin and coal shed for each dwelling.

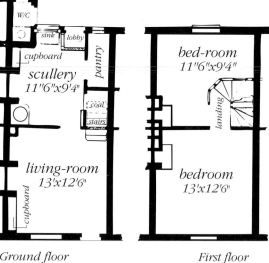

Ground floor   *First floor*

Through house without hall or parlour.

Attic floor

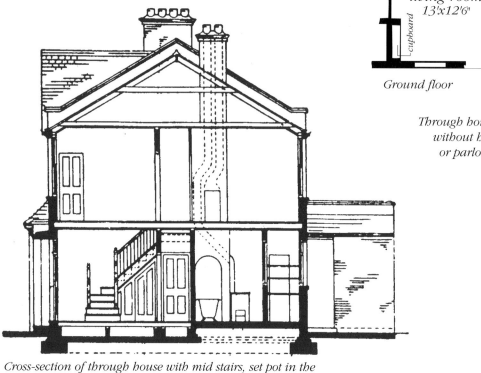

Cross-section of through house with mid stairs, set pot in the kitchen and small rear extension for 'wash-house'.

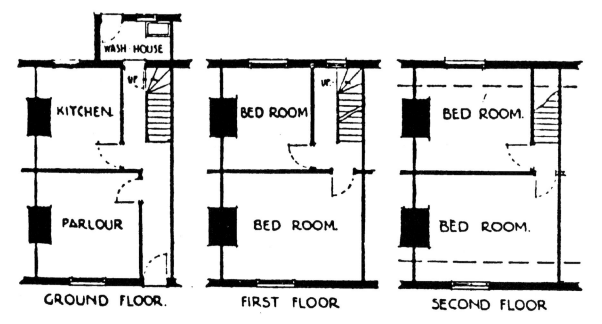

Through house with half-hall and parlour.

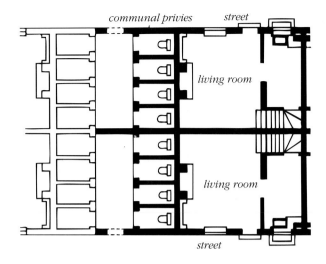

Plan of back-to-back showing end of block pair with privies for all the houses in the block.

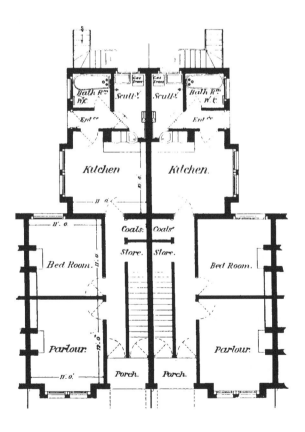

Plan for ground floors of a pair of working-men's flats. Upstairs flats had steps down to the shared yards at the back.

SEGREGATION OF THE SEXES

More and more small houses were now being designed with three bedrooms instead of two. This developed from the growing belief in the necessity of providing enough bedrooms for male and female children to sleep in different rooms.

PRIVACY

A degree of privacy actually filtered down to the living quarters of the working classes. Used to living in crowded (if not overcrowded) homes, cheek by jowl with neighbours sharing intimate affairs like privies and washing facilities, the new privacy was a relative affair.

Front doors no longer opened directly into the living-room but into an entrance passage, off which the stairs ran. This had the double bonus of securing the privacy of the lower rooms and also keeping them cleaner as the dirt from the street wasn't walked straight in. It also protected the living-room from a direct draught when the front door was opened. Windows were installed on stairs to give extra light.

Front and back doors were placed as far as possible from those of the house next door 'thus preventing, as far as possible, the evils attendant upon close proximity, which are too well known to need further comment'.

THE PARLOUR

A parlour was the height of ambition for all working-class families. For the working classes it was a social stigma to work from the home and a sign of social success to have a parlour. People saved their hard-earned pennies to decorate parlours in the style they thought fitting.

Reformers and designers of new housing preferred houses with a second living-room, scullery or wash-house because the space was then used every day. But the new inhabitants contorted themselves into the back room to create a parlour at the front.

The parlour was kept sacrosanct for special occasions. On Sundays, the whole family would gather together for lunch, the one leisurely meal of the week.

During the week, the parlour would be shut up with the blinds down to stop the carpet fading. Often it contained furniture, such as a varnished dining table, chairs and matching sideboard, bought on hire purchase. An upright piano was another coveted item. Curios collected on holiday excursions and – by the end of the century – family photos were popular decorative items.

LATE VICTORIAN 1876–99

SMALL – *back*

WIDER BACK LANES

Bylaws took effect and wider lanes were placed between the back yards of houses. The scavengers finally had sufficient room to take away accumulated cess, ash and rubbish.

The bylaws were also successful in regulating the planning of streets so that proper services could be laid on.

Back-to-backs were now illegal in some areas, although elsewhere they continued to be built in considerable numbers. They, too, were now laid out in a planned street development.

Cold Water	Hot Water	Kitchen Range	WC	Gas
yes	copper only	possibly	unlikely	possibly

Rear elevation showing a small rear extension which housed the facilities: WC or privy, wash-house, ash and rubbish bins.

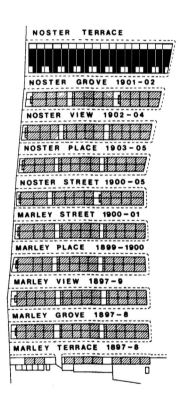

The final phase in the life of the back-to-backs: proper street development. Turn-of-the-century streets in Leeds, the last city in which they were allowed to be built.

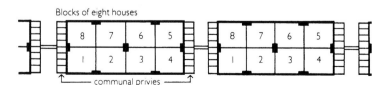

Street plan from Leeds, where back-to-backs survived into the twentieth century. Regulations limited the density of building to blocks of eight. The privies were in communal blocks situated in the gaps between the blocks.

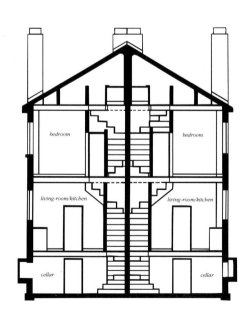

Cross-section of a late nineteenth century back-to-back.

102

street

house | house | house | house

yard | *yard* | *yard* | *yard*

b a c k   l a n e   (g i n n e l)

yard | *yard* | *yard* | *yard*

house | house | house | house

street

house | house | house | house

y a r d | *y a r d* | *y a r d* | *y a r d*

b a c k   l a n e   (g i n n e l)

y a r d | *y a r d* | *y a r d* | *y a r d*

house | house | house | house

■ *privy*

After the 1875 Public Health Act, small houses were laid out with back lanes (also known as ginnels) that allowed vehicles easy access to the rear to collect dust, ash, cess and rubbish.

EXTRA AMENITIES

The better working-class homes had other extra amenities. Fireplaces were installed in at least two of the bedrooms, even if they were only lit in times of childbirth or illness. In the belief that working-class people would not be able to afford to own items of furniture such as wardrobes, larger closets were built in to provide more storage room and to help to keep their houses tidy.

Larders and fuel stores began to be standard features. A coal shed outside meant that coal no longer had to be kept under the stairs.

More houses were given water closets and baths, and there was a move to place the privies inside the house for greater privacy and to prevent the water in the cistern freezing. Baths were usually placed in the scullery and covered by a wooden lid when not in use. In superior workers' houses the bath was placed in a separate room.

GARDENING

Gardening was considered a healthy recreation for workers. Many employers who built houses for their men supplied them with a garden or offered tenants the opportunity to take up an allotment. Having a garden was also seen as a good way of augmenting their income if they were out of work.

BACK YARDS

To improve the health of the occupants and cut down on the appalling death rate in the back-to-backs, the 1875 Public Health Act specified minimums for back yards and rear access. This ensured more room for the ash pit, a coal shed and privy or WC, which was becoming a real possibility.

Some yards now even had room for the man of the house to sit outside 'with friend and pipe'. Vegetables were grown in any spare space.

Embellishing the much-sought-after parlour.

EPILOGUE

INDIVIDUALITY AND BEAUTY

The last quarter of the nineteenth century had seen a sea change in both style and attitudes. No longer was any one form seen as correct. The middle classes were newly assertive; their choice of form had become a statement of their independence and their own views.

Red-brick and vernacular styles were an outward expression of this. Classical forms remained and were themselves a statement of orthodoxy.

LARGE AND MEDIUM

Both large and medium embraced the new forms with their corresponding improvements in plan and services. Large terraced houses were becoming the exception rather than the rule.

Basements were becoming rarer. There was a movement towards the back of the house as the garden became very sought after and more pleasant. Progress in plumbing, drains and services had made this possible.

BYLAW HOUSING

Propelled by more effective legislation in the form of local bylaws, small houses were developing a style of their own. It had been a period of improving living conditions for those who could make ends meet. This time, the gain was made possible not by wage rises but by greater spending power, due to less expensive goods and building materials.

Right: Leisure 'activity' in the back garden for those who could afford large or medium houses with good drains and services.

Above: It had become possible for the middle classes to add a degree of style and individuality to functionality; for example, a coal scuttle with a Sunflower motif, the symbol of the Queen Anne Revival.

All the working class could aspire to was functionality: a mangle for drying washing (right).

EDWARDIAN 1900–14

The Edwardian period effectively lasted from the turn of the century until the beginning of the First World War in 1914.

FORTUNES

Britain's industrial rivals were still gaining ground, but both the population and the overall wealth of the nation continued to grow. However, specific businesses, such as building, were subject to the vagaries of the marketplace. It was an era of accelerating change in many ways.

Meanwhile, people continued to be concerned about making their homes healthier. On the philanthropic side, national and local government persisted in schemes for workers' housing. But the vast majority of new small houses were still produced by the 'spec' builder.

The Edwardians were free from many of the restrictions of their predecessors — their lives and homes had both figuratively and literally lightened up and opened up. However, people still lived within a formally-ordered pattern governed by etiquette. The upper classes had long taken it for granted, the middle classes had worked for generations for it and now many working-class families finally participated by getting the separate parlour they had aspired to for so long.

Formality and etiquette remained important in the house.

Developments such as Port Sunlight (above) had cast a positive light on to the problem of workers' housing. Numerous designs were put forward, but speculative builders were still responsible for the vast majority of small houses built during the period up to 1914.

The diversity of architectural forms continued, ranging from various vernacular and 'Old English' to an equal diversity of classical choices.

The 'Old English' form

A NEW GROUND PLAN

The movement to the suburbs stretched further and further out from the town centres. At the same time, the servant problem intensified. These developments led to radical changes in the ground plans of the houses then being built.

The suburbs reached so far out that the new large suburban houses were only distinguishable from the original rural houses by their location, rather than their design. Medium houses also benefited from wider plots and improved services. Electric trams hastened the proliferation of working-class suburbs and so the small Edwardian houses were also of a better quality.

Large suburban townhouses – only distinguishable from rural by their location rather than their design.

Advertisement for a new garden suburb – with co-operation between the developer and railway companies.

GARDEN SUBURBS

The enthusiasm for Domestic Revival ideas filtered down the social scale into the repertoire of the 'spec' builders. Significant features of the Queen Anne form – for example, the striking white banding – disappeared and were replaced by Old English features. These Arts and Crafts-influenced forms were often expensive to produce because of the detailed work necessary.

House designed by the architect C F Voysey, whose work included many features that were copied by the spec builders. Only features that were economical to build entered the spec builders repertoire.

One design movement became very influential. This was the Garden Suburb Movement, which in theory aimed at mixing different classes of housing in a pleasant, semi-rural environment.

FULL CIRCLE

At the same time as some people were attracted to homes in the various vernacular forms, others distinctly preferred the classical. The most widespread form of classical building was a direct revival of the late Georgian. Their traditional virtues of clean, elegant lines, effective use of space and relative economy of construction, which had made them so popular with speculators, builders and occupants in the late eighteenth century, had the same appeal at the beginning of the twentieth. The neo-Georgian features and designs were a great success in the marketplace, bringing the architectural story full circle.

Neo-Georgian large

Neo-Georgian medium

Neo-Georgian small

LARGE – *front*

ECLECTICISM

The diversity of architectural forms continued, ranging from the various vernacular – red brick, white rough cast and Old English – to an equal variety of classical choices.

A DIFFERENT LOOK

The larger building plots in the suburbs allowed architects and builders to produce houses that were wider and lower. Consequently, the appearance of these houses had a strong horizontal emphasis. At a glance, they might appear smaller, but these new suburban houses were as big, if not bigger, than their earlier equivalents.

COMMON FEATURES

As well as the horizontal emphasis, the basement had totally disappeared and the service rooms were placed at the side. Vernacular and classical features were often combined in one design. For example, warm red brick, white rough-cast at first-floor level, casement windows with small panes either leaded or with heavy wooden transoms, semi-circular fanlights, projecting hoods, dormer windows, red-tiled roofs and tall chimneys could all be included in one design. Despite the mixture of features, the overall design was symmetrical.

A red-brick suburban design incorporating vernacular details (such as gables, tall chimneys, moulded brickwork, etc) with neo-Georgian (windows, hooded dormers).

Houses with their own driveways, such as this example from Hampstead Garden Suburb, were only townhouses by virtue of their surburban, rather than rural, surroundings.

A house in a Birmingham suburb of a similar design (to the top right).

Entrance front of a large suburban house.

Return of Georgian features: red brick, fanlight for the main entrance, small window panes, hooded dormers and door hoods for the service entrance; first floor picked out in rough-cast plaster.

WHO LIVED THERE?
The power of the traditional landed aristocracy had been in decline since cheap grain imports had begun to arrive in the early 1870s. The 'new money' came from finance, which blurred the social distinction between the middle and upper classes.

THE HIGH GAME OF CLASSICISM
The period before the First World War saw an entire range of classical designs as architects and decorators employed by the rich rediscovered the 'High game of Classicism' *(Sir Edwin Lutyens).*

The large houses were designed in a variety of classical forms at unprecedented expense. Stone, the ultimate extravagance in a brick area, was used on neo-Adam terraces in London. Elsewhere, red-brick forms ranged from the 'Free Classicism' – which was a development of the Queen Anne Revival – to the pleasantly-proportioned and versatile neo-Georgian.

Classical terrace built in stone with rustication and quoining.

Neo-classical interiors showing panelling and plaster ceiling decoration.

LARGE – *plan*

NEW GROUND PLANS

The greater width meant continuing variation in the floor plans. On the ground floor, the hall had grown in importance and was usually placed centrally as a focal point of the house. It was used as a reception room and a less formal sitting-room.

INGLENOOK

The hall now had its own fireplace, which might be the grandest in the house. These fireplaces became the core of a pseudo vernacular tradition – the 'inglenook'. Sometimes this fireplace was situated on an outside wall despite the obvious heat loss – appearance was evidently more important than comfort. The larger hall also made it possible to make more of the stairs. Often they began with a couple of broad steps, then turned for effect. Posts and fretwork screens were a further embellishment.

Upstairs, numerous rooms were placed around the central landing.

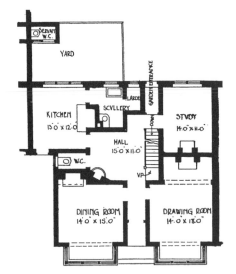

Ground floor

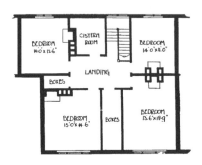

First and second (attic) floors.

An Old English living-room with exposed beams, inglenook and polished floorboards.

Plans of house with Georgian features and first floor picked out in rough-cast plaster. Note double-fronted, square plan.

House with entrance front (first floor).

House with entrance front (ground floor).

Traditional dining-room in oak with exposed ceiling beams, plate-rail and wall-panelling.

Library interior.

Neo-classical dining-room.

HALL BECOMES A PARLOUR

Nostalgia for an 'ideal' home of the remote past affected the design and use of certain rooms of the house. Instead of being a transitional entrance place, the hall became a room in its own right, inspired by the halls of medieval houses.

In the new house designs, it was given ample floor space where the family could meet together and was made cosy by a large fireplace. The fashionable desire for quaintness was achieved with window seats and inglenooks, two elements that became essential for a 'modern' house.

The new halls were multi-purpose. A common item of furniture to be found there was a writing desk. Some even had a dining area.

THE COMING OF ELECTRICITY

The installation of electricity in a house was a major aspiration. Electricity was more economical than gas, since it could be turned on and off by a switch. Neither was it dirty; curtains and carpets did not have to be cleaned as often – an important aspect as servants became scarcer. Wallpaper and paint did not become soiled and need replacing as frequently.

Electricity produced a much brighter light that could be easily diffused, so it was possible to choose lighter decorative colour schemes for aesthetic as well as practical reasons.

Overall, electric light became associated with a better class of home and was a highly desirable status symbol.

At first, the electric light bulb was such a novelty that it was left exposed, but shades were soon developed – first in copper and brass, then in glass, to diffuse the light. The light and lampshade designs of Lewis Comfort Tiffany became very popular.

GEORGIAN PANELLING RETURNS

Georgian-style panelling returned to offer a light-coloured alternative to dark, wooden Tudorbethan panelling. The neo-Georgian panelling was painted either white or in clean, pale colours.

Neo-Georgian hall with painted panelling.

LARGE – *back*

RUS IN URBES

The greater plot width meant that the service wing could be discreetly positioned to one side of the house, possibly screened off by box hedges.

The sense of 'Rus in Urbes', which had always been sought after, was now as close to reality as was actually possible. Wider lawns, large rear-facing windows and rustic features such as rain-water barrels all added to the idyll.

The back had become more desirable than the front.

To preserve the family's enjoyment of the privacy of the garden, servants' bedrooms were positioned so they overlooked the side, or even the front, of the house.

Suburban house with vernacular features: eyebrow window in the roof, casement windows with diamond pattern leaded panes, deep gables and rough-cast finish to the walls.

A calm garden layout

Cold Water	Hot Water	Kitchen Range	WC	Gas	Electricity
yes	yes	yes	yes	yes	yes

Technically, the back was referred to as the garden front.

Terrace and formal garden layout.

Pergolas and trellises were a distinctive item in the Edwardian garden. They were used to create a balance between the formal and the natural elements in the garden.

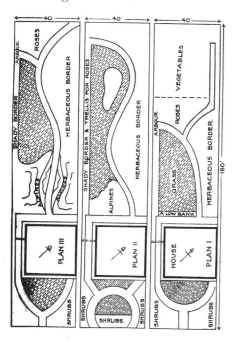

Edwardian garden plans for plots.

THE TELEPHONE

The first telephone exchange was opened in London in 1879. By 1881, there was one telephone for every 3,000 people. By 1900, more than 200,000 people in Britain had a telephone.

Telephones were seen as a convenience for the well-to-do, not something for the masses, even though the number of people who were acquiring them kept doubling.

Etiquette immediately stretched to cover the new invention. It was established that telephones should only be answered by a servant, who would then summon the appropriate person. Ideally, internal connections would link the rooms.

The first telephones were viewed as utilitarian objects at odds with home decor, so they were disguised by covering them with satin, domed cases or in such acceptable containers as adapted eighteenth-century mahogany knife-boxes.

The availability of space in the new floor plans once again allowed the inclusion of dressing-rooms. They had often been lost in the older homes when it became necessary to convert these small rooms into bathrooms.

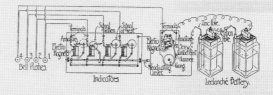

Electricity was quickly put to a variety of uses, including light, telephones and bells. Above: an electric bell system.

Rustic arch and trellis.

MEDIUM – *front*

OLD ENGLISH

The predominant form of the medium-sized house was the development of the Old English – which had originally been the rural form of the Queen Anne Revival. The success of the Garden Suburb Movement popularised this pastoral look.

Details were drawn from the same medley as in the large – and the medium also benefited from the wider plots in the outer suburbs.

The symmetry of the facade was often spread over the whole building rather than the individual house.

The red-brick neo-Georgian form grew in popularity in the years leading up to the First World War.

Pair of semi-detached houses built in 1909 with Fletton bricks and rough-cast finish. They cost approximately £425 each to build.

Pair of semi-detached suburban houses with small front gardens, rough-cast finish on the first floor and wide entrance porch.

Suburban houses built in 1911 for £550 each.

Semi-detached houses in Hampstead Garden Suburb. View from the road shows the Old English form under the influence of Voysey.

Above: Elevation.
Below left: Perspective view.

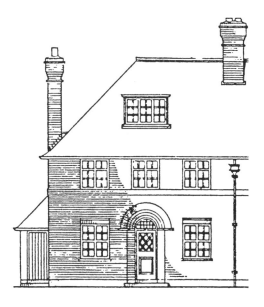

Archetypal neo-Georgian design in semi-detached form: flat-fronted, red-brick, flat-roofed dormer windows, small panes in the windows which align under each other, first-floor string course and semi-circular fanlight over the front door.

Double-fronted terraced house with dormer windows, rough-cast first floor and bay windows.

THE CLASS OF SECURITY
The middle class continued to expand in relation to the rest of the population.

The 'solid' middle class consisted of those with incomes of £700–£1000.

THE FIRST TO BENEFIT
The middle classes were among the first to benefit from the achievements of the Garden Suburb Movement. The inward focus of the new designs greatly appealed to them.

THE SERVANT PROBLEM BITES
It was the middle classes who felt the 'servant problem' most acutely. As usual, it was the lower middle classes who felt the pinch most, but it appears to have been universal among the servant-keeping classes.

There were so many other opportunities open to those who might otherwise have entered service. New jobs ranged from manning the telephone exchanges to working in light industry. Consequently, the new ground plan, with only one or two flights of stairs, was a boon to the middle-class housewife who was having to manage with less and less help from servants, full or part time.

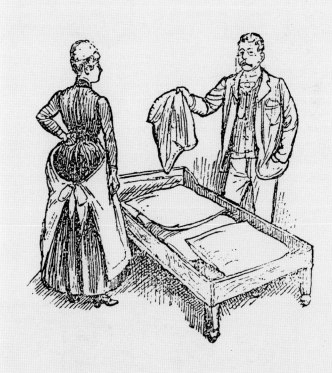

The servant problem: the middle classes were finding good servants harder to find. Consequently, better services were required from the house itself.

MEDIUM – *plan*

NEW GROUND PLAN

The outstanding consequence of the wider plot was a radically new ground plan. The medium-sized house finally broke away from the old plan of one room behind the other with flanking hall. It now adopted virtually the same sort of plan and distribution as the large.

Reception rooms were placed on either side of a central hall with a third facing the rear. Kitchen and service rooms came back into the main body of the house to such an extent that there was only a minimal need for any rear additions.

Upstairs, extra space was available for 'conveniences' such as dressing rooms, linen closets and box rooms.

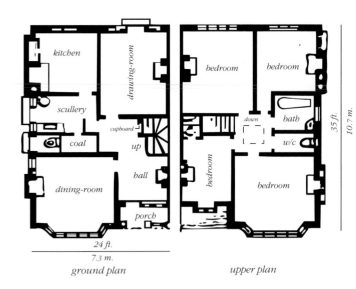

ground plan   *upper plan*

Semi-detached houses built in 1909 – they cost approximately £425 each to build. The hall has a fireplace. The kitchen and scullery are within the main body of the house. There were four bedrooms, a bathroom and a WC upstairs.

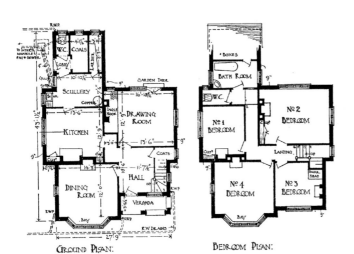

Above: suburban houses built in 1911 for £550 each, containing hall with coat cupboard, sitting-room (which has an inglenook fireplace) and rear-facing drawing-room. The kitchen was in the main body of the house but the scullery projects beyond it. Upstairs, there were four bedrooms and a bathroom.

Hall with fireplace.

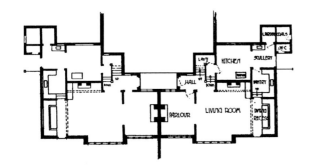

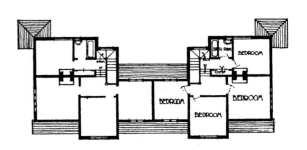

Above and right: Voysey-esque semi-detached houses in Hampstead Garden Suburb. The wide plot and plan was perhaps the ultimate development of suburban design. It could have been anywhere.

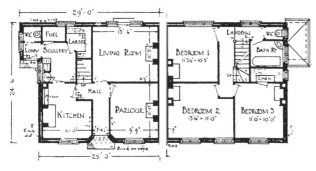

Archetypal neo-Georgian semi-detached: hall was positioned centrally with services to the left and the two reception rooms to the right. First floor had three bedrooms, a bathroom, a WC and a linen cupboard.

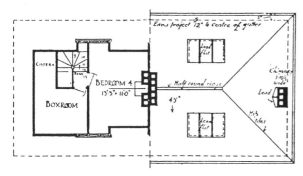

Attic floor of neo-Georgian semi-detached with roof plan showing dormer window and chimneys.

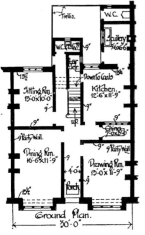

Ground floor   *First floor*

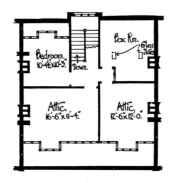

Double-fronted terraced house with central hall, three reception rooms, china cupboard. Upstairs, there were three bedrooms on the first floor, with another in the attic (right), plus a box room (which did not have a window).

THE SERVANT PROBLEM

The Victorians had complained about their servants, but by the Edwardian period availablility was the problem, not quality.

The medium-sized houses in the suburbs tended to keep only one servant and it was usually a lonely position full of drudgery. Unlike in the larger houses, there was no one for a maid of all work to socialise with and nowhere to go on her time off.

The lower middle classes were occupied with 'Keeping up with the Joneses', an American expression coined in 1913.

LABOUR-SAVING DESIGN

The growing servant problem affected the design of many aspects of the home. There was also a desire to make houses a healthier place to live. Luckily, the two aims could result in the same end product.

For example, elaborate mouldings were rejected and simple coving and skirting boards became fashionable. Parquet floors with scattered rugs replaced large carpets, or a parquetry surround was possible for those who could not afford a whole floor. Parquetry was seen as *'the ideal floor covering for health and convenience as it will never need renewing, nor beating, nor scrubbing, and…it will simplify very much the task of cleaning the room'* (Humphry, *The Book of the Home*).

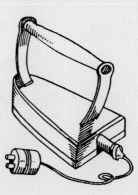

Labour-saving devices: electric kettle and electric iron.

MEDIUM – *back*

GARDEN FRONT

The similarity to the large was carried through to the back. The medium-sized house could, in fact, boast of having a 'garden front'. The pace of change was clearly accelerating when the mediums enjoyed similar benefits at almost the same time as the large.

The back was definitely just for the family and any services were carefully masked. French doors continued to be popular and there was no barrier between the garden and the house.

Doors and windows open to the garden, which rose behind this house in a semi-formal step.

A well-developed garden compensates for the modest steps down from the rear-facing bay window. The scullery extension on the right was well screened by greenery.

Voysey-esque semi-detached houses in Hampstead Garden Suburb: the back of the pair (shown above) was similar to the front.

Cold Water	Hot Water	Kitchen Range	WC	Gas	Electricity
yes	yes	yes	yes	either gas or electricity	

A pair of houses with terraces and conservatories. The left-hand house has an elevated conservatory on the first floor. The right-hand house holds its own with an awning over its terrace.

Ideally, houses were designed to face south, allowing the open terrace and first-floor bow window to get as much sun as possible.

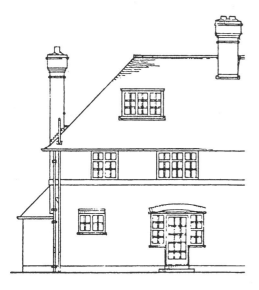

The back of the neo-Georgian semi-detached could be as flat as the front; the services could project to the side. Below: side elevation and cross-section.

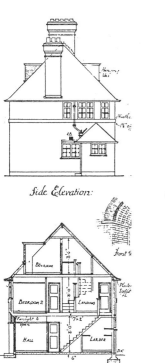

Side Elevation:

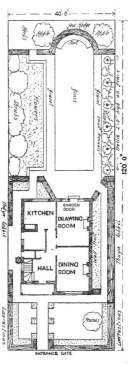

Garden design for a long narrow plot.

A small rock garden.

GARDENS

Gardens were an important adjunct to the new houses being built. The garden was seen as a place for recreation, and gardening was a healthy and respectable hobby. People, especially those who owned their houses, took immense pride in their gardens and relied on the many publications, both books and magazines, for advice on what to plant.

A gardening style that filtered down from the larger houses combined the formal and the picturesque. Suburban gardens were seen as easy, inexpensive places to entertain and alfresco tea parties became popular.

Manufacturers took advantage of the increasing number of householders with gardens and produced a great range of furniture and decorative items for them. Wooden and cast-iron garden furniture was produced on a large scale, as well as stoneware statues, urns and balustrades in a variety of sizes.

The new importance of the garden was emphasised by easy access to it from the house. French doors would lead directly into it from the main rooms at the back of the house, or into a conservatory and then into the garden.

ANYONE FOR TENNIS?

As part of the growing belief in the benefit of healthy exercise, the middle classes eagerly took up golf and tennis. These sports did not require the financial investment or social standing of the traditional activities of the upper classes, such as hunting and shooting.

The possession of a tennis court became such a social necessity that *'every wretched little garden-plot is pressed into service, and courts are religiously traced out in half the meagre back gardens of the suburbs of London, even though the available space is little bigger than a billiard table'*. This earlier statement from *The Spectator* (1884) had become even more of a truism.

Paved pathway in a London garden.

A larger plot with a tennis court.

SMALL – *front*

PROLIFERATION OF DESIGNS

There was an increasing proliferation of designs for small houses as public money became available for them. This came in the form of loans from central goverment to the local authorities. However, the vast majority of houses were still built speculatively as the local authorities could neither build as cheaply nor in anything like the quantity required.

Some of the features of the large and medium houses appeared on the small, giving the impression of some sort of family relationship between the designs which had not been apparent since the Georgian period. Warm red brick, white rough cast, casement windows, small window panes, hoods or porches over doorways, eaves, brackets and even imposing chimney stacks could all be found on this size of house. Even red-tiled roofs appeared.

As usual, in the small house the row or terrace gave the design an automatic symmetry and repetition.

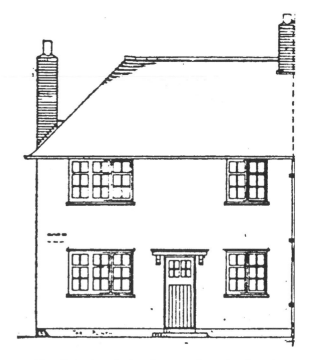

Neo-Georgian design for one of a pair of semi-detached cottages.

Working men's flats.

Neo-Georgian design for suburban cottages with rough-cast finish from eaves to first-floor level.

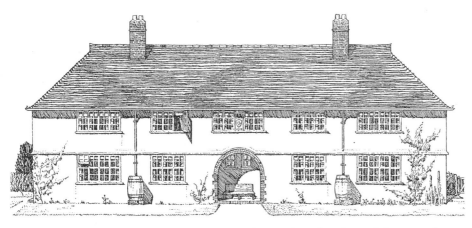

Four cottages: entrance to outer cottages were at the sides, those of the central pair were through the central arch.

1889 London County Council formed

1890 Housing Act authorises local authority house building

1900 LCC starts first major cottage estate at Totterdown Fields, Tooting

1909 Housing and Town Planning Act accepts Picturesque principles

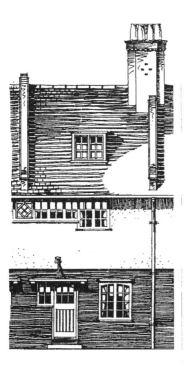

A mixture of neo-Georgian and vernacular features.

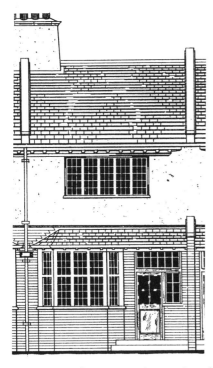

Neo-Georgian features, such as red roof tiles and window details combined with rough-cast, bay window and porch.

THE RESPECTABLE WORKING CLASS

In real terms, wages had risen for the skilled and semi-skilled workers and their standard of living improved. They worked not only in the textile and heavy industries but also in the newer light and service industries.

All the reforms of the latter half of the nineteenth century had resulted in a significant drop in the mortality rate, so the working classes were following the example of the middle classes and having smaller families. The size of the average family was now 2.5 children.

MUNICIPAL HOUSING

Reformers became more and more concerned about leaving the building of housing for this section of the social spectrum to the speculative builders, who were loath to build well for them because of the poor rate of return on their money.

To ease the congestion of working-class housing in the city centres, local authorities were allowed to buy land outside the cities where it was cheap and build on it. But the slum problem was not solved because only 'respectable' workers could qualify and afford to live in these first 'council' houses.

Prospective tenants were vetted to ensure respectability, both fiscal and moral. Neatness and cleanliness were part of the tenancy agreement and there were regular inspections to ensure that standards were maintained.

A few shillings initial key money was required and rent was payable in advance. Rents were generally 6s 6d to 9s 6d for these houses and anyone who fell a week behind was given notice to quit. Obviously, the poorest people could not afford to live in them. Ironically, the local authority was supposed to pay central goverment back with the income from the rents.

ELECTRIC TRAMS

The majority of the working class still lived within two to three miles of their work and either cycled or walked to it. By 1905, ninety-five per cent of railway passengers travelled third class, but it was the electric trams which really developed the working-class suburb.

The trams covered a larger area and were a great deal less expensive than the horse omnibus. In 1900 there were 150 tramway systems; forty per cent of them were managed by local authorities.

By the end of the period, even the trams were being superseded by the motor-omnibuses. There was an initial reluctance to realise their potential, but buses were more profitable and carried almost the same number of passengers.

SMALL – *plan*

THE LONGED-FOR PARLOUR

Many of the new designs finally gave the workers their longed-for, properly-laid parlour. The trickle-down effect that had benefited the medium continued through to the layout of working-class houses.

Improvements to the back continued and a proper water-closet was placed in the body of the rear extension, although it was reached through an outside door. Provision for bathing was made in the scullery or wash-house. Separate cupboards and built-in dressers were provided in the main living-room.

Some houses now had an effective boiler to heat water. The norm was a 'set-pot', which might be augmented by a new but economical gas ring for cooking.

Upstairs, built-in storage cupboards were also included in the house. Strenuous attempts were made to provide three bedrooms without having to enter one bedroom through another.

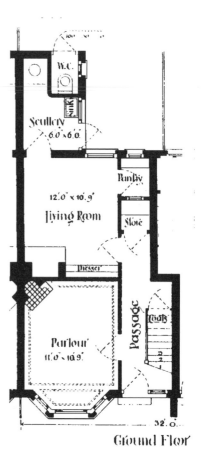

Ground floor with half-hall and small rear extension containing a scullery.

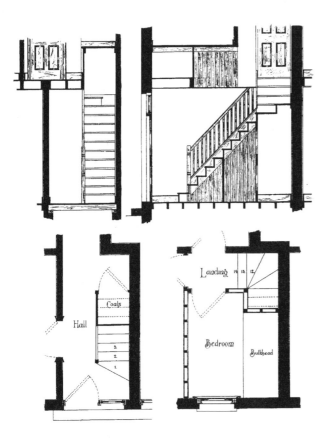

Cross-section and plans of stairs placed at the front of a small house (either in the hall, half-hall or front room).

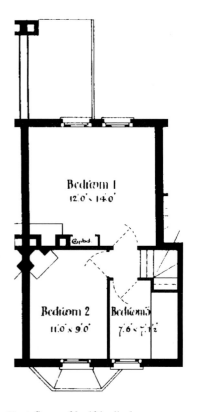

First floor of half-hall plan shown above.

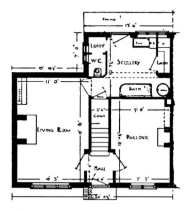

Ground floor

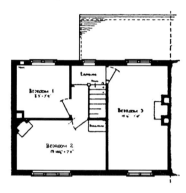

Plans for the semi-detached neo-Georgian cottages, suitable for suburban locations which suited the wider, shallower plan. Above: first floor.

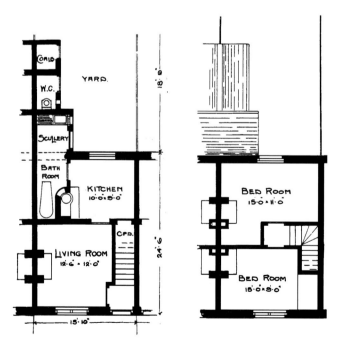

Rear extension with bath and WC. No hall or half-hall, merely a vestibule screening the entrance from the living-room.

THE BEST ROOM

The parlour continued to be a bone of contention between the designers and the tenants. The designers wanted to utilise the space available in these small houses by knocking the parlour and the living-room into one larger, lighter room. But people still wanted a separate parlour for 'best' even if it was only 10 ft by 10 ft and scarcely large enough to hold the prerequisite pieces of furniture and all the family. Although a large, light room meant a healthier environment, status was more important.

WHAT IS A HOME WITHOUT A PIANO?

Pianos, perambulators and bicycles were the most expensive and desirable items in the working-class household – the piano taking pride of place in the parlour.

THE BICYCLE BOOM

The design of bicycles was constantly improving and their price decreasing. In 1894, a new one could be bought for as little as £4.50 and there was a brisk trade in second-hand machines.

The 'safety bicycle', with enclosed chain, brakes and freewheeling mechanism, appeared during the Edwardian era.

It were eminently affordable and became known as 'the Working Man's Friend', as he could ride a bike to work at less cost than any other form of transport. Cycling also had a social side and many clubs were formed for enthusiasts.

Her first lesson

WORKING-CLASS WOMEN

As working-class men earned more, now their wives tended to stay at home and look after their own families. By 1911, about ninety per cent of married women were housewives and mothers only.

Women looking for work now had other opportunities besides textile work, including nursing, post-office work, teaching, typing and positions in the new consumer-based industries of confectionery, jams, cigarettes, footwear and light engineering like bicycle manufacturing.

SMALL – *back*

FRONT AND BACK GARDENS

The plots of small houses still usually had only the minimum for an effective back yard. At best, they might enjoy both front and back gardens.

Some houses catered for their refuse ash and coal in permanent rear extensions, while others had portable ashbins that could be placed anywhere in the yard.

An average rent in 1914 was 9s 3d per week, including rates.

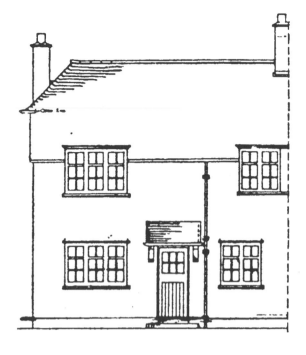

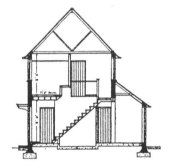

END ELEVATION.

Neo-Georgian semi-detached design. Above: back. Far left: side elevation. Left: cross-section with rear extension similar to the rear elevation shown at the top of the facing page.

Perspective View Showing The Arrangement of Houses in Terraces.

Above: architect's designs

Cold Water	Hot Water	Kitchen Range	WC	Gas	Electricity
yes	copper	possibly	yes	possibly with meter	no

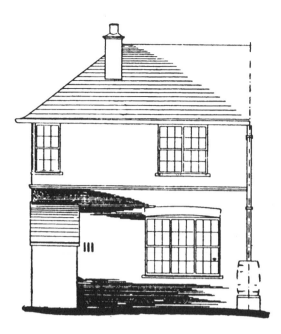

Neo-Georgian semi-detached design with rear extension (see cross-section shown on the facing page).

Detail of the rear of working men's flats, showing stairs from the top flat to the yard.

Detail of the back yards of through houses.

INDOOR WCS

The three and four-bedroomed houses built by the councils now all had an inside water-closet. In some houses, it was in the main building with an open lobby between it and the scullery for health reasons.

In other houses, the water-closet was placed in a small rear extension and could only be reached from the outside. A small percentage of the houses were built with five rooms and in these the bathroom and a separate water-closet was often installed upstairs.

BATH AND WASH-HOUSE

A variety of designs were put forward for bath and wash-house. Some were built with separate hot-water apparatus. Others, more modestly, stored the bath under the floor. Early local authority housing had a lobby entrance to the WC from the wash-house.

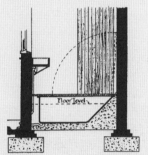

Side view from the kitchen.

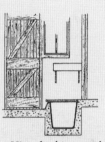

View looking at the door to the yard.

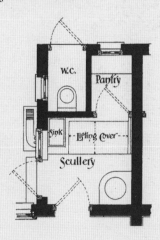

Plan of an arrangement for storing the bath under the floor of the scullery.

EPILOGUE

THE END OF AN ENTIRE ERA

The First World War (1914–18) not only marked the end of the Edwardian period, but also of an entire era in the story of the house. During the war there was very little building, but after the end of the war everything changed.

LARGE

The Edwardian era had seen the swansong of the large townhouse. Henceforward, accommodation in town for the rich would take the form of service flats in 'mansion' blocks. Indeed, existing large townhouses had already begun to be converted into flats.

MEDIUM

Medium houses would continue to be built speculatively, but for sale, not for rent. Henceforward, those who lived in them were increasingly owner-occupiers.

SMALL

The urgent need to build 'homes fit for heroes' resulted in public money being made available on a scale that could meet the need for workers' housing. It took time for this to happen. Demand for this class of house was so great that rents were fifty per cent higher than before the war for the same dwelling. At first, local councils were unable to build even the economical and more spacious neo-Georgian designs as cheaply as the spec builders had.

The problems of re-housing the poor and slum clearance were not solved until the creation of the Welfare State after the Second World War (1939-45). By that time, the Luftwaffe had arguably done more than the earlier slum clearance programmes ever did.

FULL CIRCLE

Circumstances had changed entirely, but the houses built after the First World War were in the same style as those being built when it began.

The neo-Georgian forms had brought the story full circle: from the late Georgian formula for large, medium and small came a complete range of designs which were spacious and economical.

However, in 1914, unlike the late eighteenth century, there were numerous other forms to choose from: neo-Georgian, with its classical derivation, was balanced by the other stylistic influences – particularly the Old English, which was to line the suburban highways during the inter-war years.

DETAILS

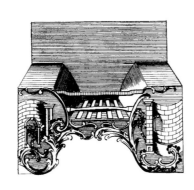

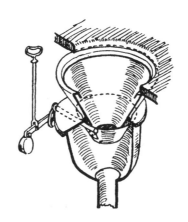

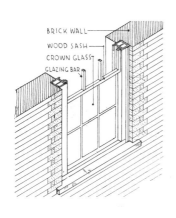

BRICK WALL
WOOD SASH
CROWN GLASS
GLAZING BAR

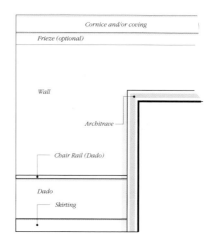

Cornice and/or coving

Frieze (optional)

Wall

Architrave

Chair Rail (Dado)

Dado

Skirting

Frets, or Guillochis of Various Sorts.

CHIMNEYS

The construction of fireplaces in all homes was essential – the main source of heating and cooking was coal burnt in open, and later closed, fireplaces. Each fireplace had its own flue to carry the smoke up through the house to the roof, where it escaped through the open chimney pot.

The layout of the flues looked complicated but was standardised throughout all the building styles. The flues were gathered together to leave the roof at the same place, thereby simplifying roof construction and weather-proofing for the builder.

Fireplaces serving the same storey were often placed back to back so that their separate flues could be carried up together. A well-designed flue was curved, not only to avoid fireplaces on other levels, but also to prevent rain and draughts of cold air dropping directly on to the fire. They are easily identified by looking up inside them – daylight cannot be seen at the top.

The correct placement of the chimney stacks on the roof was also essential to an efficient fireplace.

BOY SWEEPS

One of the many horror stories of child labour, boy sweeps were finally banned in 1829. By 1850, most sweeping was carried out mechanically, but adult sweeps could still be seen riding around on their bicycles with their brooms in 1914.

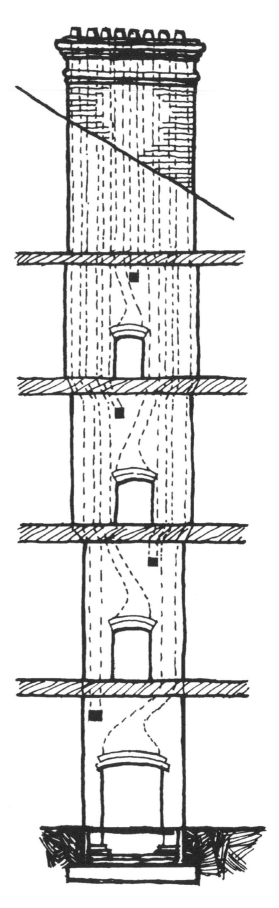

How the flues were 'gathered'. Note how the chimney breast broadened to accommodate the additional flues.

SMOKE DOCTORS

'Smoke Doctors' were applied to chimneys that suffered from down draughts – which caused smoke to be forced back down the chimney into the living space.

The conical cowl also protected chimneys from down draughts, but unfortunately prevented the necessary escape of flue gases. An alternative – the circular deflector – was more effective. Wind could bounce off its sides and chimney gases could still escape from the leeward side.

TALL CHIMNEYS

Apart from practical considerations, chimneys were ignored by designers until the Queen Anne Revival period. The chimney, a strong feature of vernacular architecture, became a prominent element as part of a symbolic return to the traditional values of hearth and home.

Architectural design now reached right up to the chimney pots and the roof line was heavily emphasised. In some new houses it was the chimney that struck the eye most forcibly.

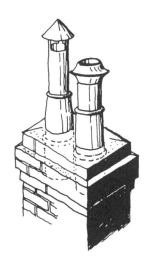

Smoke Doctors – cowls which helped the chimney pots to draw properly.

A villa design of 1870 shows the trend towards designing right up to the chimney pots themselves.

Typical late nineteenth-century chimney pots.

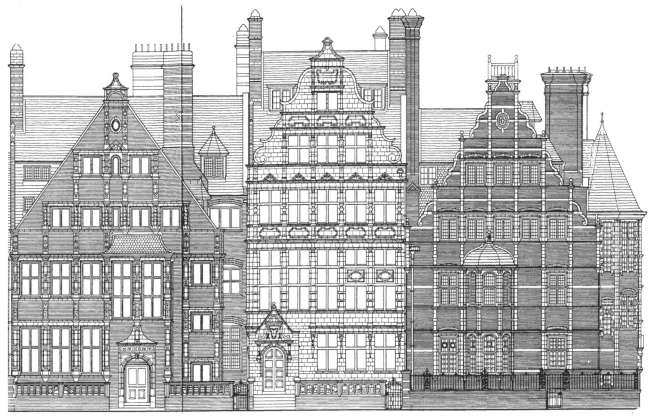

Queen Anne Revival – roof line and chimneys were an integral part of the design.

FIREPLACES

The fireplace was the most important functional item in any room until the advent of central heating. Of necessity, it also became the decorative focus. In common with other decorative features, the importance of a room was apparent from the size, design and decorative detail of its fireplace.

DEVELOPMENT OF THE GRATE

The original grates – dog grates and basket grates – were really intended to hold logs of wood. The basket grate was a metal container with legs which was placed in the fireplace recess. This simplistic design was wasteful of both heat and fuel. The baskets were usually semi-circular with classical supports inspired by Adam's designs. They were frequently made of polished steel with pieced decoration.

From the seventeenth century, coal became the standard fuel in all large towns and the hob grate, designed for coal, became more usual. The fire was enclosed by cheeks or 'hobs' that fitted into each side of the fireplace instead of standing freely in the centre. They were made of cast iron and had relief decoration on the side. The bars were made of wrought iron. The hobs were also useful for cooking and keeping food and drink warm.

COUNT RUMFORD

The American Benjamin Thomson, known as Count Rumford, became horrified by the pall of smoke that hung over London and the waste of fuel it implied. His innovations resulted in more efficient designs of the grate and fireplace, which threw more heat back into the room and used less fuel.

THE REGISTER GRATE

The result was the register grate, which reduced heat loss straight up the chimney by the introduction of a metal back and sides. The 'register' itself was an adjustable flap that allowed more or less heat to escape as desired. The addition of fire-clay retained yet more of the heat. A model of the register grate with a semi-circular arch remained popular throughout the latter part of the nineteenth century.

Basket grate

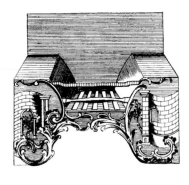

Hob grate with cheeks

The characteristic curved Victorian fireback with register.

Fireback with tiled surround

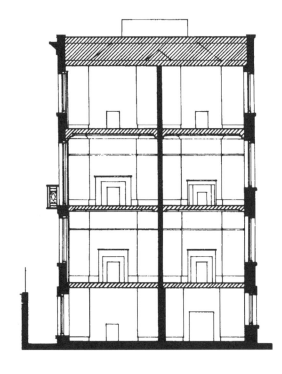

Cross-section showing the hierarchy of fireplaces.

SURROUNDS

A hierarchy of materials was used for fireplace surrounds which depended on the importance of the room.

White marble was the popular choice for main rooms, decorated with coloured marble inlay, scagliola or painted designs. Jasper-ware, ormolu and bronze or gilding were also used.

Influenced by Adam, the chimney-piece became smaller and more restrained than previously. The decoration was neo-classical with simple brackets and plain pilasters. Swags and columns were employed and the whole design followed classical proportions.

In the Regency period, the design became even more restrained and a reeded surround with simple paterae was favoured.

In keeping with the rest of Victorian decor, the surround gradually became heavier in appearance.

Decorative tiles became an important feature on fireplaces that had a register grate. They filled the space between the surround and the grate. By the end of the century, they were being mass-produced.

Large marble surrounds with brackets supporting a shelf (which usually had a large mirror on it) were popular. They gadually fell out of favour, but were expensive to replace. All kinds of ideas were developed to disguise them. The most ubiquitous was the mantle drape.

By 1900, wooden mantels rivalled marble at the top of the market. Overmantels with many shelves and bevelled mirrors had become fashionable, replacing the single large mirror in middle-class homes. The new mantles gave people a place to display bronze and brass. They were most likely to be found in Tudorbethan-style homes.

The Arts and Crafts penchant for medieval features produced larger, more open fireplaces.

HOME AND HEARTH

The Edwardian period saw a deeply emotional attitude to the fireplace as the heart of the home. Fireplaces were often grandiose, wood-burning and designed with inglenooks or cosy corners with built-in seating.

Adam-style drawing-room fireplace surround with overmantel.

Adam designs: fireplace surround (left) and grate (right).

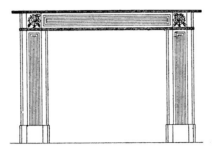

Regency fireplace surrounds with reeding and paterae.

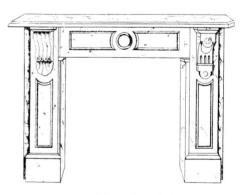

Victorian corbels – detail

Marble with corbels

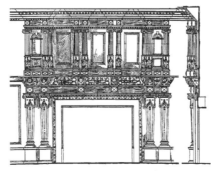

Massive overmantels

The inglenook

COOKING

Until the eighteenth century, all domestic cooking was done over an open fire in a grate, using solid fuel. The food was either heated in a pan, boiled or roasted on a spit. If less heat was required, the hob or 'cheeks' at the side of the grate were used. Coal was the standard fuel.

TRIVETS, JACKS AND POTHOOKS

Numerous useful devices were invented over the years to make cooking over open fires easier. Trivets, pothooks, jacks and cranes were used to suspend or stand pots over the fire. More complex was the bottle jack – a clockwork gadget that could turn a joint or a pot. Gradually, cooking space was increased and made more flexible by inventions like the Dutch oven, a free-standing container that was placed in front of the fire. It had an open front and a reflective surface behind.

RANGES

'Ranges' began to appear in the 1780s. The fire was still open, but a 'slider' was introduced to regulate the size of the fire according to the number of pots being used.

A swinging crane suspended pots over the fire, often including one which provided a constant supply of hot water.

Cooking in an open domestic grate.

Trivets were used to make miniature hobs over an open fire.

Open range with crane and built-in cupboards on either side.

An open range in use

THE NEW KITCHENERS

The influence of Count Rumford was felt 'downstairs', as well as 'upstairs'. Appalled by the sheer inefficiency of open cooking fires, he produced the first design for an enclosed range – the 'kitchener' as it came to be called.

Kitcheners were rapidly acknowledged as being more efficient and cleaner, and became highly desirable. Cooks liked them and stayed in households where they had been installed.

Although by the 1840s completely closed ranges were being installed in large houses, kitcheners developed gradually as manufacturers began to offer numerous improvements on the open ranges. Transitional half-enclosed forms were quite common in the years either side of 1850.

The closed range continued to come into wider and wider use The basic design and method of cooking on them remained the same until around 1900 when alternatives to solid fuel began to be utilised.

These alternatives took the form of appliances like gas rings and electric kettles. However, progress was slow – the coal-burning, enclosed range was still the norm in 1914.

Half-closed range with boiler and oven.

Fully-closed range.

Count Rumford, pioneer of the kitchen range, the register grate and numerous other advances in cooking and heating.

A kitchen in 1874: Dutch oven and fully-closed range.

COOKING

COPPERS

Boilers specifically for heating water were fitted separately, as well as in combination with a kitchen range. These separate boilers were often referred to as 'coppers'.

Large and small houses were more likely to have separate boilers. Medium-sized houses tended to use combined ranges to heat water or, after 1869, some sort of appliance in the bathroom, such as a geyser.

The appliances in the large houses varied from coppers for washing clothes and linen to systems which heated water for the entire house. In the last quarter of the nineteenth century, the price of gas was cheap enough to allow gas-fired coppers to rival coal-fired.

SETPOTS

Small houses used 'setpots' to heat water, usually situated in the corner of the back room on the ground floor. Consequently, this room was often known as the wash-house.

The setpot consisted of a hearth with a flue. The copper – a metal container – fitted over the fire and was covered by a wooden lid. The copper lifted out for filling and emptying. The hearth was either open or equipped with a 'soot-door'.

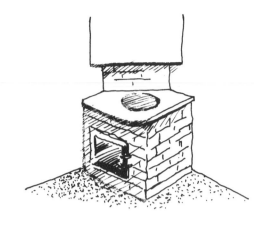

The setpot: a boiler with flue situated in the corner of the back kitchen.

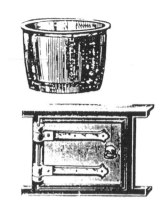

The removable copper held the water. The fire door was an optional, ready-made feature.

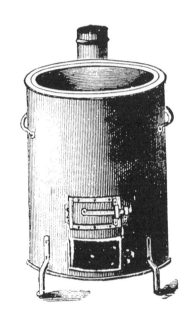

A copper for heating water and washing.

A maid using a copper.

Portable gas stoves

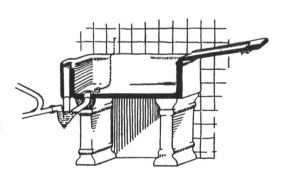

The deep sink with draining board, known as the butler's sink, was used for washing-up – especially for china and glassware.

HOT-WATER SYSTEMS

Complete hot-water systems first appeared in the 1840s. Obviously, they were expensive to install, run and maintain, which made them the province of the rich.

By the end of the century, hot-water systems began to be installed more frequently, though they were still likely to appear only in larger houses.

KITCHEN SINKS

Originally, sinks were placed at the front of the house. As water pressure and drainage improved, sinks moved to the back, where they were installed in the scullery or wash-house.

In large houses, sinks were sometimes installed on landings outside the bedrooms. These shallow sinks were known as slop-sinks or housemaid's sinks. Strictly speaking, a slop-sink was equipped for the disposal of the contents of chamberpots.

The larger, deeper sinks were known as butler's sinks or scullery sinks.

As plumbing improved, sinks were fitted with traps and disconnected from the main drains.

DRESSERS

Dressers and a table were the standard furniture of any kitchen. They were itemised among the fixtures and fittings when the house was rented. They were usually made of softwoods, such as pine, and were painted.

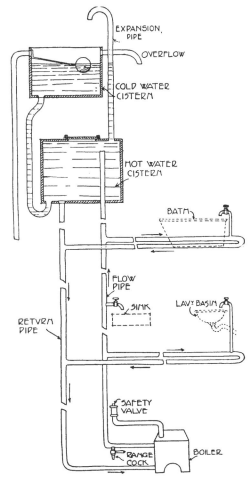

ILL. 164. THE TANK HOT-WATER SYSTEM.

An ambitious Edwardian hot-water system

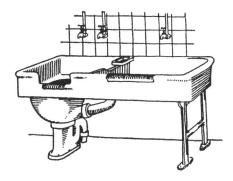

The housemaid's sink was a shallow sink intended for slops; in its fullest form, it had a plumbed-in water-closet for emptying chamberpots.

An Edwardian kitchen dresser

BATHING

Before the advent of piped supplies, all water had to be carried into the house from the nearest stream, conduit or pump. This was especially onerous in the townhouses with their many floors. The carrying was, of course, all done by servants. Personal washing was conducted in the bedroom using a ewer and a basin.

Having a bath was an occasion. Baths were portable and were brought into the bedroom or, in the case of the lower classes, into the kitchen, scullery or wash-house. If possible, a bath was taken in front of a fire.

In the late eighteenth century, piped supplies of water were provided by private companies and were only available for a few hours a week. Soap was bought by the pound in large blocks. It was often eked out with cheaper materials such as washing soda.

PIPED WATER

During the Georgian period, piped water began to be laid on, but only intermittently. The water pressure was so low it could barely reach from basement to ground floor.

By the Regency period, the water supply had become more efficient. Pressure was improved so that it could reach higher than the ground floor.

In fashionable circles, cleanliness began to be associated with elegance. The servants in houses with new, closed kitchen ranges, which enabled water to be heated and piped round the house, were the lucky ones.

Efficiently-piped water enabled a permanent bathroom to become a possibility. It would be located upstairs. Small bedrooms or dressing rooms were converted and installed with some of the new 'bathing' fixtures. Shower attachments to baths were common.

Those without a bathroom upstairs continued to bathe in the bedroom, kitchen, scullery or wash-house.

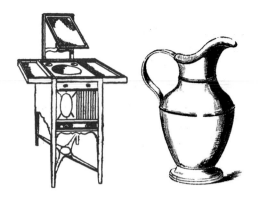

Above left: Washstand design by Sheraton. Above right: Ewer – the basic way to carry water.

Wash sets: Ewer and basin (shown) and other items including the chamberpot.

Washstand with ewer and basin; other items included the chamberpot.

A more utilitarian form of bath, with carrying handles, which might also be used for laundry.

Above: The hip bath – a very common form. Right: With shower attachment.

Family bath time in 1861

WATER SUPPLY	
1810	Steam engines for pumping
1827	Cast iron mains (allowed higher water pressure)
1829	Water-filtration and reservoirs

Municipalisation of supply	
1847	Manchester
1876	Swansea 100% supply *'except in midsummer'*
1878	Liverpool 100% supply
1880	London still only 50%
1902	London finally 100% supply

By the third quarter of the nineteenth century, large houses had a bathroom in their original plan. At first, they were decorated in the same way as the other rooms in the house. Despite the effects of water and steam on wallpaper and floor coverings, baths and hand basins were panelled-in like normal furniture.

However, concern for hygiene was growing due to successive epidemics.

SANITARY BATHROOMS

In 1871 the Prince of Wales nearly died of typhus, attributed to 'bad plumbing'. Public awareness of hygiene became acute and 'sanitary' became the buzzword.

Baths and washbasins were now enamelled with rolled tops, and all pipes were exposed for easy cleaning. The new, powerful gas-fired 'geyser' emitted clouds of steam, so walls and floors began to be tiled. Glazed tiles were perceived to be more hygienic. They greatly enhanced the level of cleanliness and were responsible for the increasingly distinctive look of the bathroom.

LUXURY

Bathrooms became ever more sophisticated and luxurious. In the Edwardian era, the bathroom benefited from a vast range of decorative innovations and appliances, including heated towel rails, showers and splash-backs for the handbasins.

The bath was now fully enamelled, and tiling was de rigeur and fitted to a height beyond which water could not reach. Windows too were designed and glazed to maintain privacy.

Virtually all medium-sized houses were built with bathrooms conveniently near the bedrooms. Most new small houses still had to manage with the wash-house, kitchen or scullery.

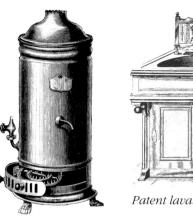

Gas geysers emitted clouds of steam.

Patent lavatory (handbasin).

Sanitary handbasin (known as a lavatory).

Panelled patent baths – seen as 'a cheap and useful luxury'.

Left: A novel but highly dangerous idea for those who had gas installed was to heat the water in the bath itself – the 'General Gordon' even had a towel warmer.

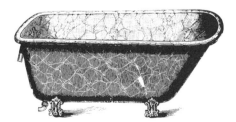

A japanned, roll-top bath.

The splendour of the Edwardian bathroom – with adjoining WC.

WCS AND PRIVIES

EARLY WCS

The water-closet as we know it developed from designs patented in the 1770s. The designs produced by Cummings and Bramagh had a cistern, pan, valve and water-trap. They were originally intended to eliminate the foul smell which came back up the open pipe from the sewer or cesspit.

These early pan or valve types were complicated, liable to become dirty and needed constant maintenance.

They also used an unprecedented amount of water, which was expensive and sometimes caused flooding around the house until it became legal to connect them to the local sewers (1810 in London).

HOPPER AND WASHOUT

Improved designs followed; first the 'hopper' and then the 'washout'. These utilised the new 'S' trap, which was simpler and cleaner than the dreaded 'D' trap.

Hoppers were cheap and therefore considered suitable for servants and the working classes. But their spiral flush was weak and the pan was too narrow at the bottom and inevitably became fouled. The washout had an effective flush but also became soiled.

WASHDOWN

The culmination of all these developments was the pedestal washdown, which had a large flushing rim, a large water area and a hinged seat. The discharge flowed into the drain without fouling the pan.

Made of a single piece of ceramic, it was free-standing – hence 'pedestal'. It conformed with the emphasis on sanitary fittings: it was clean, open to inspection and easy to maintain.

By 1914, the pedestal washdown with syphonic cistern and intercepting trap was state of the art.

A further improvement followed in the Edwardian period. The syphonic washdown acquired a high-level cistern. It was quieter and had a powerful flush due to the syphonic action of the vertical downpipe.

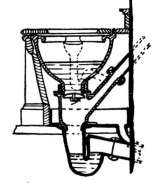

Pan type WC.

Early pan and valve types: complicated, dirty and in need of constant maintenance.

Left: The long hopper had a weak flush. Right: A cheap option.

The pedestal washout – complicated but using an S trap.

The short hopper with S trap.

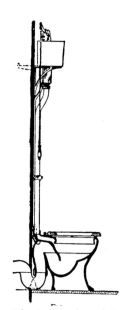
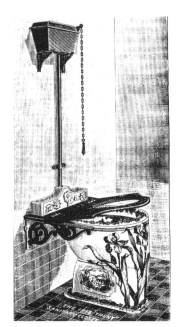

The pedestal washdown with syphonic cistern.

CISTERNS

The contents of the straightforward valve cisterns were flushed when the chain was pulled. The water was only released while the chain or lever was held down.

The syphonic cistern developed at the same time as the washdown. A single pull emptied the cistern. These cisterns had a characteristic domed top, which accommodated the top of the flush pipe. This was enclosed in a cylinder that was raised by pulling the chain. The water was drawn up above the level of the flush-pipe and started the siphonage that emptied the cistern. The ball-valve then allowed the cistern to be refilled to a level just below the top of the flush pipe.

INTERCEPTING TRAP

The intercepting trap prevented the smell and gases from the main sewer coming back up into the house (the original reason for the WC itself). This had been at its worst in terraced houses, where the sewer ran beneath the dwelling.

The intercepting trap placed an effective waterseal between the house and the main sewer. It also provided a means of inspecting and clearing blocked drains or the build-up of potentially explosive gases.

PRIVIES

Those who did not have WCs used privies. Privies took a variety of forms: bog-house, pail and earth closets.

The pot or pail used as a receptacle was later empied into a cesspool or 'midden' heap. The cesspool or midden should in turn have been regularly emptied by the nightmen, and the pots and pails cleansed and disinfected.

When this failed to happen, the consequences were disastrous. Sadly, this was often the case when access to the yards was difficult.

Earth closets were a patent form which used dry earth or sawdust to deodorise the sewage. The earth was discharged into the pail afer use. They provided an alternative when local sanitary arrangements failed to provide a water-borne system.

The valve cistern.

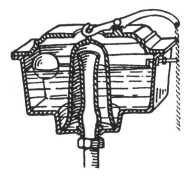

The syphonic cistern.

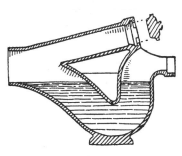

The intercepting trap sealed the house from the main sewer.

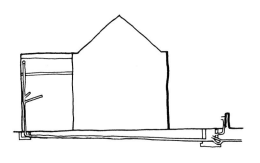

The run of the drains showing the location of the intercepting trap.

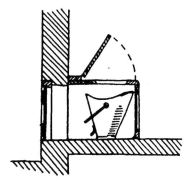

A privy using a pail.

A galvanised pail.

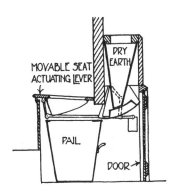

An earth closet automatically discharged earth into the pail when the user stood up.

LIGHTING

CANDLES

Candles were the basic form of lighting until the 1880s. They ranged from expensive beeswax, which scarcely dripped and was odourless, to cheap and smelly rush dips.

Rush dips were two foot by four inch strips of common rush dipped in animal fat and clipped into a holder. Eleven rushes cost $\frac{1}{4}$d (a farthing) in the 1780s. Each dip lasted an hour.

Tallow candles were better. They were also made from animal fat – usually mutton. Each cost $\frac{1}{2}$d and lasted two hours. Constant trimming was needed as they burned badly and gave little light. They were commonly used by artisans and the middle class.

Beeswax candles were extravagance itself. Reserved for special occasions even by the rich, they were the only kind suitable for chandeliers because they required less attention.

Chandeliers, an exclusively upper-class fitment, were suspended from a hook in the ceiling and lowered to the floor for access. They were a highly conspicuous display of affluence when the norm was no more than two candles to a room. It was usual to carry candles from room to room, except on formal occasions.

EARLY GAS

Gas began to gain acceptance only after its adoption in the House of Commons in 1852. The early gas burners gave about five times as much light as a candle when turned up and were used in combination with candles and lamps. However, they emitted a lot of soot and were noxious. Ceiling roses were developed to catch the soot and decorating colours had even more reason to be dark to hide the dirt. As gas was poisonous, it was considered unhealthy for bedrooms. Also, the light was harsh and cast unflattering shadows.

Candle = 1
Oil Lamp = 3
Gas = 5
Incandescent Gas Mantle = 10
Electric light bulb (pre 1907) = 10
Electric light bulb (post 1907) = 16

A modest interior lit by candles.

Chamber candlesticks with shade (top) and snuffer (below).

Candles and gas were used in combination.

Candelabrum

Paraffin oil lamps became the usual way of lighting parts of a room well.

A gas wall sconce.

140

A gas wall bracket.

GAS v RIVALS

Paraffin (mineral) oil lamps seriously challenged gas in the 1860s. Gas came back with the incandescent burner in the 1880s. This gave twice as much light as the earlier 'fish-tail' burners. It was also more efficient, which meant it could be turned down and consequently gave off less smoke. Unfortunately it produced a rather green light.

Incandescent burners were as bright as early electric light bulbs. The problem of shadows was solved by the 'inverted' burner. In the 1890s, penny-slot meters brought gas light within the range of the working class. Gas still had the advantage of being cheaper than electricity.

Despite the disapproval of the experts, gas gained ground over its rivals until the arrival of the incandescent electric light bulb in 1907.

ELECTRICITY

Electricity also arrived during the 1880s, at the same time as the new gas mantles. By 1900 it had become a serious rival, gaining the high ground – the approval of the experts – because it was clean, odourless and efficient. These qualities appealed especially as the price came down.

It was, however, no brighter than gas until the arrival of the incandescent electric light bulb in 1907. These bulbs were the brightest to date, giving out the equivalent of a 25 watt bulb today.

Electricity companies canvassed street by street to gain enough subscribers to lay on supplies. Electricity became a prominent feature of advertising for new housing, increasing its association with a better class of home; an association reinforced by its choice for prestigious developments such as Hampstead Garden Suburb.

By 1914, most new large and medium houses were being fitted with electricity, but there was still fierce competition. The cleaner, brighter light resulted in lighter, more delicate decor and colours. More easily adapted to pendants, electric appliances began to acquire their own character rather than resembling gas fittings.

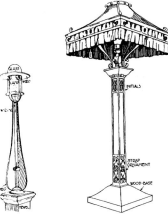

Inverted gas burners avoided the harsh shadows thrown by an upward flame.

Incandescent gas burners were twice as bright.

Early electric fittings resembled gas fittings. Gradually they acquired a distinctive look of their own.

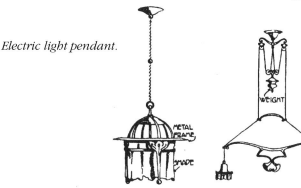

Candlestick lamps.

Electric light pendant.

Adjustable light fitting with counter-weights.

WINDOWS

By the late eighteenth century, sash windows were the standard for townhouses. Eight or twelve panes were common and the glazing bars were quite substantial.

Local building fire regulations were stringent: windows, because they were made of wood, had to be fully recessed behind a reveal that was eight inches deep or two courses of brickwork.

Shutters were fitted to filter sunlight. Internal shutters were more common than external, except in small houses, which were more concerned with security.

In large and medium houses the sashes were 'hung'. In small houses, where they were often unhung, they had to be chocked open or closed.

Plate glass arrived in 1832. For the next fifty years, windows were subdivided into, at most, four panes. Glazing bars became thinner. With plate glass came French doors, allowing easy access to balconies and verandahs.

From the 1840s, windows became an architectural feature. Surrounds were emphasised, and pediments and brackets were added, creating the appearance of miniature temples, known as aediculae.

The rustic Italian form grouped windows together in twos and threes. This greatly eased the problems of alignment of doors and windows, which resulted from the modular, Palladian approach.

During the early 1850s, the taxes on windows and glass were abolished. Bay windows became both popular and prestigious. It was easy to align windows above the bay; pairs or windows with margin lights fitted neatly above.

PERENNIAL WINDOW TYPES

The shallow segmental arch came from vernacular architecture. It was the cheapest and easiest way to build a window arch.

The Venetian window was an imposing combination of three windows with a pediment over the central one.

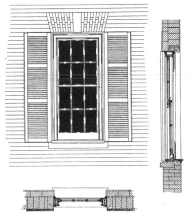

Sash window with external shutters. Cross-section (right) and plan view.

Sash window with semi-circular top to upper light.

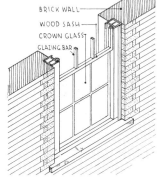

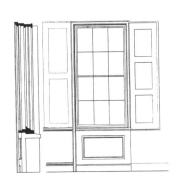

Sash window seen from the inside, with internal shutters. Cross-section (left).

Sash window with Gothic detail.

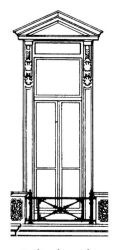

Aedicula with French doors.

French doors seen from the inside.

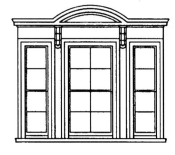

Venetian window

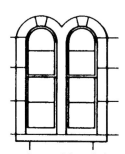

Pair of round-headed windows in the rustic Italian form.

RADICAL TRANSFORMATIONS

Queen Anne Revival ideas had a profound effect on window design. Glazing bars and small panes came back into fashion. The emphasis on individuality resulted in as much variation as possible.

Vernacular forms such as the oriel were revived and every other existing form was employed. The casement, hinged at the side, returned as a noticeably vernacular feature.

Regulations were significantly relaxed in 1895. Windows no longer had to be so deeply recessed and surrounds were allowed to project.

Casements were more fully employed. Sashes were modelled on early Georgian examples.

This emulation of early Georgian classicism was further enhanced by a return to thicker glazing bars, small panes and projecting surrounds.

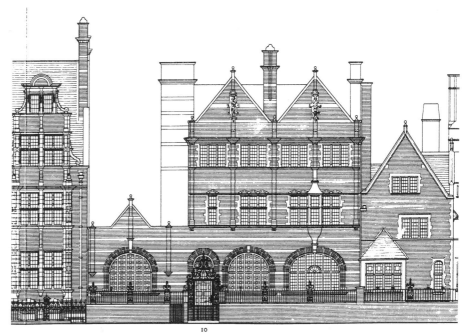

Window detail was a strong characteristic of the Queen Anne Revival.

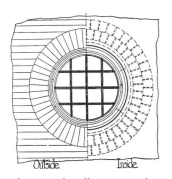

The round Bull's eye window.

Casement windows made a comeback. Early twentieth-century example in metal.

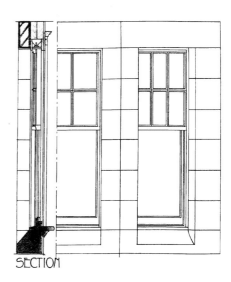

Economical design for medium houses: detail on the top light only.

Edwardian forms: dormer (left), segmental arch over casement windows (right).

Edwardian classicism: segmental arch over sash windows (left), casement windows with small traditional lights tucked under the eaves (right).

External doors were made of hardwood in large and medium houses. Internal doors were of softwood and painted.

Initially, small houses were unlikely to possess hardwood doors unless they faced the street. As small dwellings improved, they too benefited from stronger, smarter hardwood doors.

The mortice lock and pocketable keys had recently become available in the latter half of the eighteenth century. Typical Georgian doors had six panels.

After 1774, wooden doorcases were banned as a fire hazard. They disappeared for over a century. Projecting decoration had to be made of more fire-proof materials such as Coade stone. However, the fanlight survived, becoming a more distinctive feature once doorcases were no longer fitted.

FANLIGHTS

The purpose of the fanlight was to provide natural light for the hallway. The semi-circular shape gave the fanlight its name. The tracery, which enhanced this effect, was often ironwork and provided delicate embellishment. This remained true even if the fanlight was of the larger but less distinctive rectangular form.

Regency fanlights were distinguishable by having a flatter curve than the semi-circular Georgian ones. Following the development of plate glass in the 1840s, a large fanlight without tracery became standard until the 1870s.

WATERSHED IN DESIGN

The 1840s proved to be a watershed in the development of the door: letterboxes first appeared and four-panelled doors became the most common type.

By the 1860s, as basements became less common, doorways were set back inside the house. This gave them more shelter, as well as making them look more imposing. This feature met with so much approval it was adopted for virtually all large and medium houses, whether they had a basement or not. One obvious development was the pairing of front doors, corresponding to the pairing of the rear-extensions.

Georgian front door with round-headed fanlight and six-panelled door.

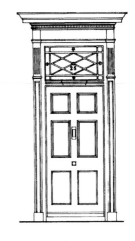

Georgian front door with rectangular fanlight and six-panelled door.

Regency fanlights were depressed.

Victorian front door with full portico, rectangular fanlight and four-panelled door.

Victorian medium doors were distinguished by the pairing of front doors and recessed porches.

Queen Anne Revival with ironwork detail and lights in the upper panels.

Re-introduction of the porch hood.

Twin doors of a pair of working men's flats.

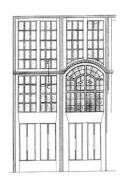

Detailed glazing of the upper panels continued into the Edwardian era.

Edwardian doors had deep lower panels and small lights in the upper panels.

SWEETNESS AND LIGHT

The Queen Anne Revival broke up the uniformity of the doors themselves. The two upper panels of the door were often glazed. Fanlights and margin lights benefited from an approach which centred on variation and detail. Small panes and intricate glazing designs were used in combination with stained glass 'lights'.

The panelling of the doors themselves began to change around 1900. The new styling consisted of a solid panel, subdivided vertically, surmounted by six small panes of glass.

Hooded porches reappeared as part of the neo-Georgian look.

INTERNAL DOORS

Internal doors followed the same development as external. Six panels were typical until the 1840s, thereafter four. Towards the end of the century, light woods such as yew or ash were used and left unpainted, in step with the trend towards a lighter look. After 1900, there was a great deal more variation in the number and proportion of the panels.

Small houses often only had ledged doors internally and perhaps for the rear entrance, WC or privy. They would have been made from softwoods, usually pine and painted.

DOORS FITTINGS

As usual, the grandest rooms had the best fittings – handles, escutcheons and finger plates. These were usually made of brass, although porcelain and china were also popular.

The variety of designs available increased with the advent of mass production during the nineteenth century. Once again, choice was assisted both by the increasing circulation of catalogues and the development of builders' merchants and retailers.

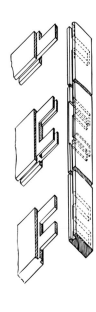
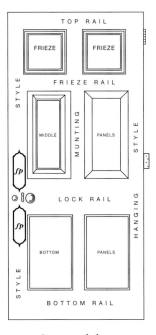
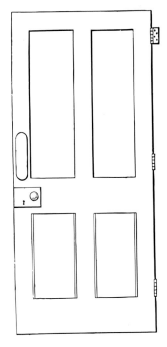

Construction of the joints of the door.

Six-panel door.

Four-panel door.

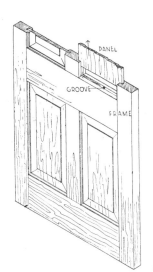
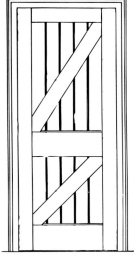
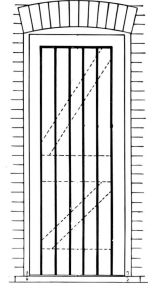

Inside of a ledged door.

Outside of a ledged door.

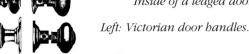

Left: Victorian door handles.

Left: Regency door knockers. Above: Victorian door handles, finger plates and mortice locks. Right: An elaborate design for an Edwardian door handle.

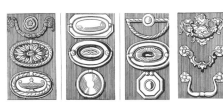

Georgian handles and plates.

BRICK AND STONE

BRICK

The two main building materials were brick and stone. Brick was cheaper and available everywhere. The other reason for the widespread adoption of brick was its fire-resistant qualities. It became the principal building material from the late seventeenth century. Its use in polite architecture at that time also helped to popularise it.

Bricks were made locally, sometimes even on site, in the Georgian period. The colour varied acording to the local 'earths'. There was a definite pecking order: 'best', 'good' and 'common'.

'Stock' brick usually implied good quality and was used as 'face' bricks on the exposed outer surfaces. Inferior 'place' bricks were used on the inside and party walls. The best bricklayers did the face work; apprentices took care of the place work. Expensive coloured brick was often used only on the facade, particularly for medium-sized houses.

BONDS

The structure of a brick wall demanded that the various layers be locked, or 'bonded' together for strength. Various patterns were developed for this purpose. English bond was one of the earliest. Flemish bond was, for a long time, almost universal.

The headers laid across the course were meant to ensure the courses were locked to each other. Rat-trap bond was another form that created a kind of cavity wall. This offered some degree of insulation and saved a few bricks.

JERRY BUILDING

Builders often adopted a penny-pinching attitude to their work. The result was usually bad brickwork: 'snapped' headers meant weak or non-existent bonds for the sake of saving a few half-bricks. This was so rife in the Georgian building industry that even the experts condoned it. It was still frequent in the second half of the nineteenth century. Snapped headers were perhaps the most notorious form of 'jerry building'.

Map of England and Wales showing brick and stone areas.

English Bond (below)

Flemish Bond (above). Ideally there should have been four courses measuring a foot in depth including the mortar,

BRICK TAX

Brick was taxed with varying degrees of severity between 1784-1850. This had the effect of standardising the size of bricks. The result was a brick which varied from 3¾ins to 4½ins in width by 8ins to 9ins in length. The depth of a brick varied from 2ins to 3¼ins.

PATTERN AND COLOUR

Decorative effects were easy. Patterns were made by using different coloured bricks. Bricks could also be cut or mouded in imitation of classical details and string courses.

Window arches were an important structural and decorative feature – and a guide to the quality of the building. Tapering bricks were originally created by 'rubbing' – a skilled and, therefore, expensive work. Later, machine-made bricks and moulded terracotta ornament became widely available.

COLOUR

Colour was subject to fashion. Choice became ever wider as catalogues advertised varieties of brick nationally; these were then distributed by rail. Hitherto, only locally available colours – reds, blues, yellows and browns – were used as detail and surface decoration. Polychromy became a real possibility, even for small houses, after the middle of the nineteenth century.

STONE

Stone was more expensive and usually more prestigious. If it wasn't available locally, it was too expensive, except for limited use in details such as lintels.

The top of the line was 'ashlar', smoothly-finished blocks that fitted tightly and neatly together. A cheaper alternative was to use ashlar for facing but filling in behind with roughly-dressed stone, rubble or brick.

Stone also varied in colour from locality to locality. Portland was grey, but Bath was sandy.

Classically-influenced architecture inclined towards stone if affordable. Even when this was impossible, the appearance of stone was desirable; hence the use of stucco, particularly during the Regency period when brick was discredited.

Brick cornice with gutter.

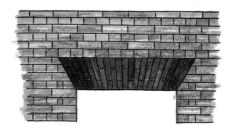

Straight window arch.

Window with segmental relieving arch.

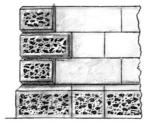 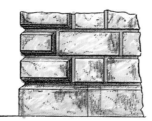 

Stone: Ashlar with worm-holing (left), rustication (centre) and dressing terminology (right).

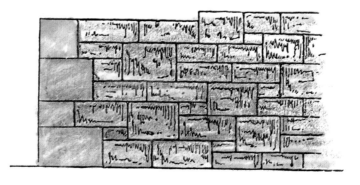

Stone: Squared rubble walling.

COLOUR – *Georgian*

INSIDE

The most significant characteristic of the Georgian approach to colour was that certain colours 'set off best with one another'. There were definite dos and don'ts as far as combinations were concerned.

Georgian interiors were as colourful as the materials available allowed. Pastel blues and greens were common for newly-plastered walls, resulting from mixing copper or iron sulphate into the plaster to deter mildew. The taste for pastel colours remained long after its origin had been forgotten.

Colour treatments reflected room use, reinforcing the hierarchy of rooms within the house. For example, lighter and softer schemes (such as Lake or Rose Pinks) were employed for drawing-rooms, a dark Sea Green for dining-rooms.

'Fancy' colours were available, but were more expensive because they had to be made from scratch. These were, therefore, reserved for details.

Some Georgian interiors relied on fixtures and fittings for colour and used 'drab' as a neutral background. Marbling and graining were widely admired and used effects.

OUTSIDE

Ironwork and railings were painted black or steel blue. Doors were green or blue. The fashion for windows was moving away from 'white' glazing bars to a dark brown – painted or 'grained'.

Stucco (plaster) was invariably painted to imitate stone. Shade varied according to the colour of the local stone.

Bricks were made locally and so their colour was usually the result of the materials available. Fashion was moving away from red stocks, which were always the most expensive. Brown was becoming the most common.

WHITE

Georgian 'white' bore no resemblance to modern 'bleached' or brilliant whites. It was an 'off' white, and was often referred to as 'stone'.

Above: Green was a popular colour for drawing-rooms. Right: Hallways were often painted in 'stone', one of the cheaper 'common colours', reflecting the hierarchy of rooms within the house.

Common Colours

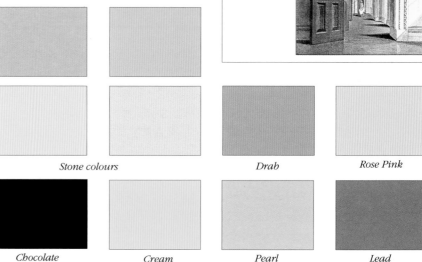

Stone colours   *Drab*   *Rose Pink*

Chocolate   *Cream*   *Pearl*   *Lead*

Fancy Colours

Sky Blue   *Walnut*   *Sage Green*   *Dark Green*

Mineral Red   *Sea Green*   *Olive Green*

Combinations to be avoided at all costs
GREEN/BLACK   BLACK/UMBER   RED/BLUE/BLACK

Left: Smalt, a prohibitively expensive dark blue colour made from crushed blue glass, cost almost five times as much as a 'common colour' (19d a square yard compared to 4d for a 'common colour').

COLOUR – *Regency & Early Victorian*

INSIDE

The archetypal Regency colour was red, 'a proper tint of crimson'. This was often used in drawing-rooms in combination with gold. Red was acknowledged as 'the best ground for pictures'. There was also a new range of orange reds.

Green was also still popular in the drawing-room, bedrooms and libraries.

Yellow was a controversial colour. Strong use of yellow was liable to be criticised – even the Duke of Wellington wasn't immune.

Drabs were still common. Although new 'bleached' whites were becoming available, they were seldom employed in house painting and were deemed 'bad taste'.

From the 1830s, there was a trend towards lighter colours – lilac or fawn in combination with bright green.

Stripes, the best-known Regency feature, first appeared as wallpapers. After 1824, stripes became available in fabric form.

Gilding was used to enliven the woodwork. Skirting boards were painted chocolate brown.

OUTSIDE

The Regency palette was altogether more daring and comprehensive.

External railings and the new verandahs were painted 'antique bronze' (green with powdered copper dust added).

Doors were always painted, unless they were mahogany or oak; good wood was proudly displayed, the rest concealed.

Window glazing was predominantly dark, often grained.

Door surrounds were painted 'stone'. Stone colour now followed fashion. For example, in London, stucco was painted to resemble Bath stone rather than the more local Portland.

Brick was associated with poor-quality housing and industrial building. Consequently, it was covered by plaster whenever possible. Grey 'galt' bricks were an acceptable alternative.

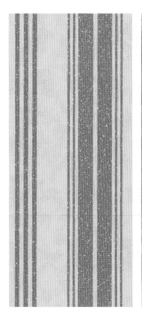

Above left: A Regency stripe in 'a proper tint of crimson' and gold exemplified the stronger use of colour in the early decades of the nineteenth century. During the 1830s there was a trend towards lighter colours.

Above right: The picture room of a great house showing the use of a 'picture gallery red' as a background colour for displaying works of art.

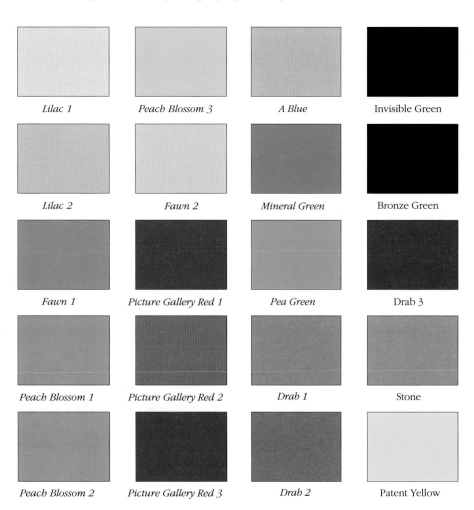

Lilac 1	Peach Blossom 3	A Blue	Invisible Green
Lilac 2	Fawn 2	Mineral Green	Bronze Green
Fawn 1	Picture Gallery Red 1	Pea Green	Drab 3
Peach Blossom 1	Picture Gallery Red 2	Drab 1	Stone
Peach Blossom 2	Picture Gallery Red 3	Drab 2	Patent Yellow

COLOUR – *Mid–Victorian 1851-75*

INSIDE

The period from the mid century to the end of the 1870s was distinguished by deep, rich 'almost womb-like' colours:

> *'Our atmosphere clamours for sealing-wax reds, deep oranges, clear yellow and beautiful blues'*
>
> (Mrs Panton, 1869)

A new generation of chemical dyes had arrived which fed this appetite for bright colours. A rich opulence was created by using different colours together in similar shades.

The dark impression given by mid-Victorian interiors was the result of this method of using colour. The colour schemes – combined with the dirt resulting from open coal fires and the dim level of light from sooty gas lighting – were dark and oppressive.

Heavily-patterned papers appeared above the dado in deep shades of green or burgundy.

The nature of different rooms was still discernible but by other means, such as pictures: oil paintings for the (masculine) dining-room and library; tapestries and water-colours for the feminine rooms like the drawing-room.

OUTSIDE

There was an emphasis on colour and surface decoration: detail and ornament were the key elements.

In 1861, Prince Albert died. Railings were painted black in mourning for Queen Victoria's husband. Doors might also be black or were painted in dark, rich colours. Window frames were generally dark, grained or bronze green. Stucco was still stone coloured. Barge boards were dark in colour.

Stained glass was just beginning to make an impact on fanlights and margin lights.

Above: A Mid-Victorian interior.

Below and right: The Victorians liked bright colours, but the way they used them together made their interiors look dark.

Deep Green

Sage Green

Prussian Blue

Burgundy

Gold

Crimson

Plum

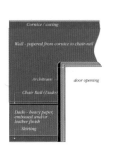

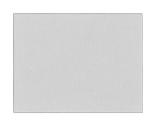

Deep Orange

Clear Yellow

Sealing Wax Red

COLOUR – *Late Victorian 1875-99*

INSIDE

The designers of the Queen Anne Revival, led by William Morris, used plum, sage green, rose, gold, ochre and Prussian blue.

In the 1890s, white as we know it came into favour for the first time and cream, the contemporary version of drab, returned to the fray. The result was a considerable lightening of the overall look.

Traditional English woods, such as oak, yew and elm, were employed so that even panelling – which echoed Tudorbethan models – looked lighter.

Those imitating neo-classical elegance actually painted their woodwork white.

Dining-rooms, however, still remained dark and masculine, but were less cluttered by furniture.

OUTSIDE

Red brick was the hallmark of the newly assertive middle classes. Moulded ornament in warm terracotta and hanging tiles reinforced the warm look of the facade of the house. Horizontal features were painted white.

External woodwork and windows were also picked out in white. Although commonplace to twentieth-century eyes, this was a radical departure from nineteenth-century practice.

Those who eschewed the Queen Anne style and stayed with conservative, classical forms continued to choose grey bricks which resulted in a distinctly cool look.

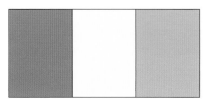

Terracotta/Cream/Rose

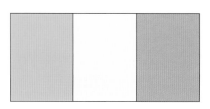

Yellow/Cream/Drab

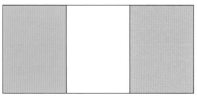

Old Gold/White/Pale Blue

Plum/Cream/Red leather

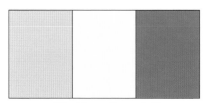

Lilac/Cream/Peacock Blue

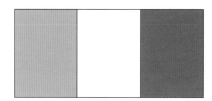

Drab/White/Chocolate

Prussian Blue/White/Crimson

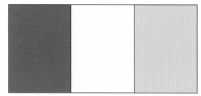

Olive Green/Cream/Salmon

The adaption of the sunflower signified artistic awareness and was used widely on houses as an external decorative motif, particularily in terracotta.

COLOUR – *Edwardian*

INSIDE

By the early 1900s, internal colour schemes were lighter still. Paler tints were becoming both more popular and more practical.

In general, colours remained in keeping with the type of room. The hall was resplendent in greens, blues, terracottas and 'Old Gold'.

New 'enamel' paints appeared that were suitable for light-coloured finishes. White enamel became popular for the panelling, which was once again being installed in halls as the neo-Georgian revival gained sway in the suburbs.

A typical colour scheme for the dining-rooms of these houses would have been red and gold with yellow and white ceilings and cream-coloured cornices.

The drawing-room would be more delicate in sparrow's egg blue, embellished by stencilled or painted rush and grass designs.

The price of painting and decorating fell in the years leading up to 1900 and fluctuated thereafter. Consequently, no spring cleaning was considered complete without a change of pattern and colour.

OUTSIDE

White horizontal banding was no longer the prevalent style. Windows, however, continued to be picked out in white. White rough-cast appeared on the upper floors.

For the Old English look, the infill between the gables was also white. The gables themselves were picked out with black 'timbers'.

Red continued to be the predominant colour of facing brick, particularly in the final years leading up to 1914.

The characteristic black and white gable of the 'Old English' look (medium).

Pale Blue

Terracotta

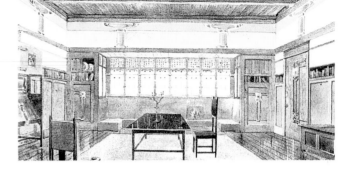

New materials included water-based paints in wide ranges of colours, with numerous 'biscuit' colours and greys.

 *Pale Yellow*

 *Golden Yellow*

 *Rose*

 *Mauve*

 *Maroon*

 *Chocolate*

 *Neutral Brown*

 *Terracotta*

 *Brick Red 1*

 *Brick Red 2*

 *Stock Brick*

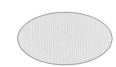 *Pale Buff*

 Pale Sage Green

 Dark Sage Green

 *Pale Green*

 Light Stone

 *Blue Green*

 *Peacock Blue*

 *Azure*

 Pale Grey

 *Indian Grey*

 *Stucco*

 Light Drab

Lilac

PAINT EFFECTS

INTRODUCTION
Paint effects were used throughout the entire period, both on walls and woodwork. Only good wood was left exposed, otherwise it was painted.

Paint effects were subject to the dictates of fashion and the prejudices of the marketplace. As an effect was practised more widely, it moved down-market and the standard of execution tended to drop. Consequently, it lost its appeal at the top end of the market. Each class avoided anything they thought their 'inferiors' were doing.

GEORGIAN
Marbling and graining were fashionable. Plastered walls were a recent development and awaited the attention of the paintbrush. Ceilings were sometimes painted to resemble clouds. Painters were reknowned for their 'three colours', which were actually darker and lighter tints of the colour itself.

Outside, stucco was given colour washes 'three times in oil' – the cost was 8d a yard, 1s if sand was added.

REGENCY
New effects joined the repertoire; 'flame' was the most notable. A range of ceiling tints replaced cloud ceilings during the 1820s.

VICTORIAN
The stringent attitude to painting anything that wasn't mahogany or oak resulted in a plethora of fake finishes, often poorly executed.

Pianos – essential to a well-equipped house – should have been walnut. If not, they were inevitably grained.

QUEEN ANNE REVIVAL
Graining became anathema to the up-to-date. Cast-iron baths and fireplaces were frequently japanned – covered by a marbling effect.

EDWARDIAN
Stencil effects were favoured by the middle market, especially grass and reed designs. Friezes, made of paper or stencilled, were very popular. Painted effects provided an alternative to wallpaper and plaster borders.

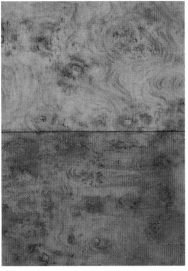

Graining: root of oak. Note the simulated 'join' between two different pieces of wood.

Graining: maple.

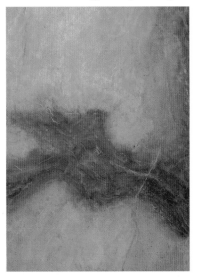

Marbling: alabaster.

Flame – a form of woodgraining.

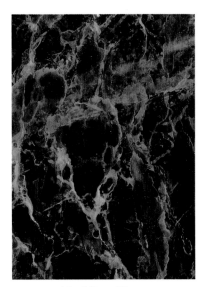

Marbling: Tinos.

Marbling: Rouge Roi.

PATTERNS

Late eighteenth-century patterns came from both classical and vernacular traditions. There was also a certain amount of Chinese and oriental influence.

Many classical decorative motifs were disseminated through pattern books. These were usually executed by the craftsmen themselves in plaster, paint or wood. Flowing designs, such as swags and flowerpots, were used for plasterwork and fireplace surrounds. Numerous geometrical patterns, reminiscent of classical antiquity, were applied both to paving and cabinet work.

Wallpapers were still printed on small sheets and were relatively expensive. Even so, there were numerous patterns available, including many vernacular motifs: oak stems, leaves, acorns, Tudor roses, lattice-work, teardrops, sprigs and snowdrops.

The predominant mood was light and graceful, in a decidedly rococo vein.

HAMILTON WESTON WALLPAPERS

Floral design c. 1775.

HAMILTON WESTON WALLPAPERS

Found in Bath.

Found in Archway House.

Classical detail: swags and flowerpots.

Swags and flowerpots applied directly on to the wall itself.

Rose-tinted walls with, by 1790s standards, an extravagant carpet design.

HAMILTON WESTON WALLPAPERS

Mid-eighteenth century, found in Twickenham.

Handbill for a late eighteenth-century wallpaper company.

Frets, or Guillochis of Various Sorts.

Guilloches and fretwork with paterae: these examples were originally for ceiling decoration.

Original fragments of Georgian wallpapers.

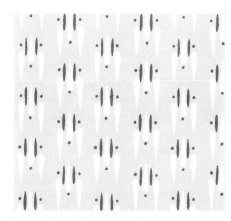

Strand Teardrop c. 1790.

The design of this eighteenth century paper shows a distinct Indian influence.

Above: Swags and paterae on a pale blue background, with additional fretwork decoration on the walls.

Chinese-style wallpaper.

PATTERNS

Regency patterns were similar to their predecessors. The main difference lay in the new approach to colour, which was stronger and more brilliant, and in the rapidly advancing technology.

Fabric and wallpaper production changed drastically. Patterned fabrics, particularily stripes, were widely available from the 1820s. Wallpaper printing changed from wood-blocks to fully-mechanised large-scale production by the 1840s.

The mid-Victorian period was distinguished by the arrival of aniline dyes in 1856. These were chemical dyes made from coal tar that provided the rich colours so popular at the time. Flock wallpapers were at the height of their popularity. 'Velvet' papers were top of the range.

It gradually became apparent that some of the materials used in these colours were toxic. The worst offender was green, which used arsenic and was known to be poisonous.

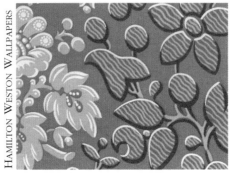

Swakely c. 1820.

Stripes became brighter and stronger during the Regency period.

Anthemion (honeysuckle), a frequent Regency motif derived from ancient Greek forms.

Husks: detail used by Adam.

Gadroons: Detail for edges and borders.

Kingston Market c. 1820.

Hedgerow, an early cylinder printed paper of 1830-40.

Border papers: Late eighteenth and early ninteenth century.

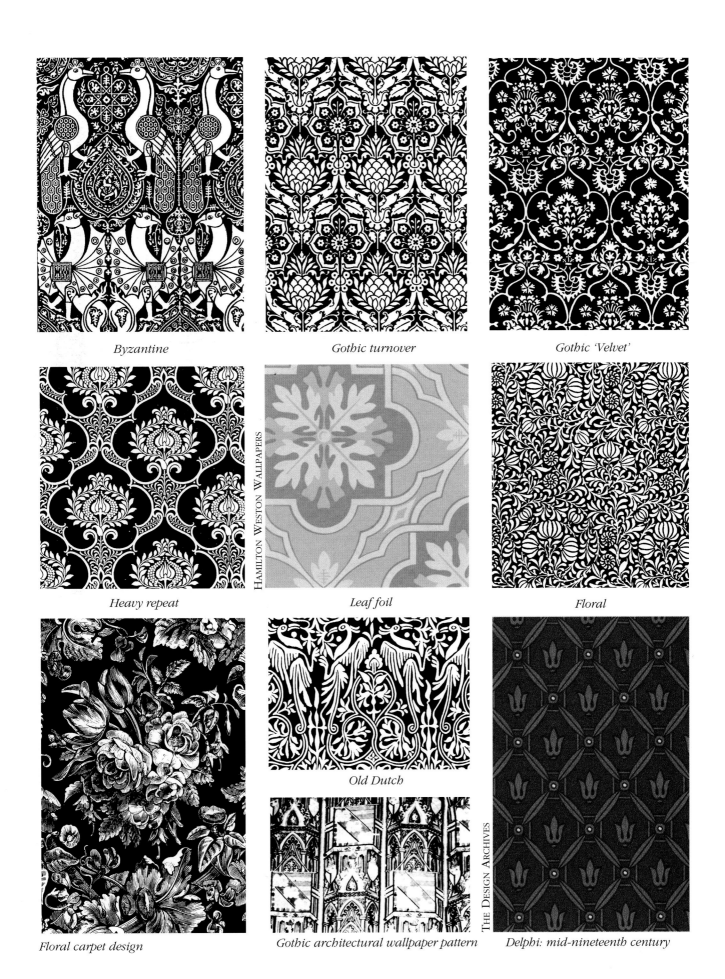

Byzantine

Gothic turnover

Gothic 'Velvet'

Heavy repeat

HAMILTON WESTON WALLPAPERS

Leaf foil

Floral

Floral carpet design

Old Dutch

THE DESIGN ARCHIVES

Gothic architectural wallpaper pattern

Delphi: mid-nineteenth century

PATTERNS

By the end of the century, 'sanitary'-coloured papers and fabrics were proudly advertised. The non-toxic nature of the products was a prominent part of the sales pitch.

Special patterns for children appeared that shared the lighter, brighter characteristics of the period.

Ready-made products for walls and ceilings proliferated. A complete range existed, from fully-moulded plaster to heavily-embossed paper facsimiles.

Borders and friezes became prominent again.

Ceiling roses.

Plaster ceiling borders.

Plaster ceiling designs.

Daisy, a William Morris design.

Acanthus, by William Morris.

A workshop making fibrous plaster details.

Michaelmas Daisy, Morris & Co. 1912.

Carpet design involving palms, cacti and scrolls.

Acorn, by William Morris.

Trellis, a William Morris design.

Colour scheme used by the architect Voysey in his own hall and dining-room.

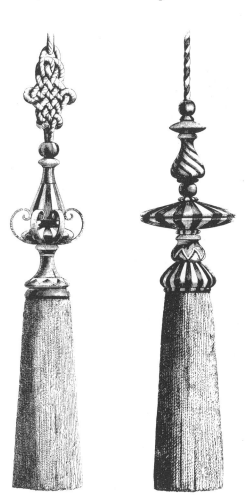

Decorative bell-pulls.

Carpet pattern: ferns.

PATTERNS

Stencilling took pride of place among decorating techniques in the Edwardian era.

Details such as swags, flowerpots and other moulded details reappeared, providing frequent evidence of the neo-classical revival which was then underway.

A stencil design: pride of place among decorative techniques.

Neo-classical moulded wall panel.

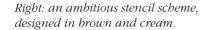

Right: an ambitious stencil scheme, designed in brown and cream.

Two frieze designs: the top one is based on the book The Water Babies *by Charles Kingsley.*

By the late nineteenth century, a wide range of ready-made stencils were available to order in metal or paper form.

Above left: Flowerpot stencil designs.

Above right: Borders.

Right: Advertisement for a stained-glass manufacturer's products.

Nursery design for colour printing or hand painting.

Stained-glass design circa 1901.

Walter Crane illustration.

TILES

Glazed and unglazed tiles were a traditional feature, both indoors and outdoors. They were used in specific areas of the house – kitchens, conservatories, hallways and, later, bathrooms. Tiled hearths and grates were also popular.

The great expansion in the use of tiles came in the 1850s after the invention of the encaustic tile in 1840. Encaustic tiles were produced by inlaying different coloured clays which then fused together when fired.

Geometrical patterns were produced using the natural colours of the clay – white, cream, black and red. This suited the contemporary emphasis for detail and surface decoration. Blue, green and lilac became available after chemical dyes were introduced in 1856.

Ceramic tiles greatly increased in use during the 'sanitary' era, especially in bathrooms, because of their hygienic and decorative properties.

By the late 1870s, tiles were being used in halls up to the dado rail. The range of designs expanded to include Middle Eastern patterns and motifs. Later, the undulating patterns of art nouveau also appeared as glazed ceramics, especially in porches, fireplaces and hallways.

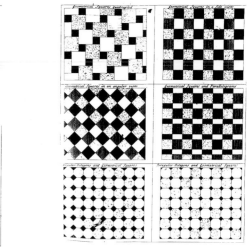

Geometric patterns from an eighteenth-century pattern book.

Above and below: Encaustic tiles – reproductions of traditional geometric patterns and borders, from Orignal Style by Stovax Limited.

Design for encaustic wall tiles.

Design for encaustic floor tiles.

Italian tile design.

A pattern built up with multiple tiles.

ORIGNAL STYLE BY STOVAX LIMITED

ORIGNAL STYLE BY STOVAX LIMITED

Printed tiles - Left: Corner, border and an individual tile which was used to add interest and variety within a geometrical pattern. Right: single tiles and a pattern built up from 12 tiles.

MOSAIC TILE FLOOR

INLAID TILES

INLAID TILES

PLAIN TILES

DECORATIVE WALL TILING

PLAIN TILES

Glazed ornamental tiles from the Pilkington Company.

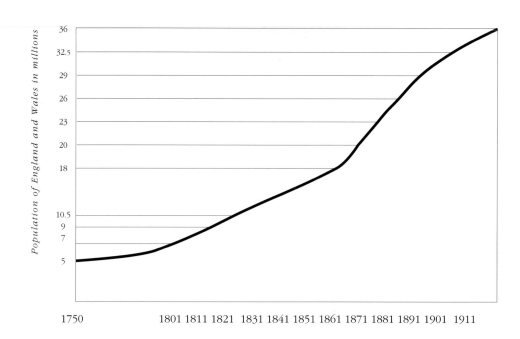

Year

Earlier figures are based
on surviving records,
such as Parish Registers
of births, marriages
and deaths

1700	5 million
1750	5 million
1765	7 million

ANNUAL PERCENTAGE GROWTH

1774–1800	**0.9%**
1811–12	**1.3%**

BACKGROUND

The population level remained steady from 1700 to 1750. But due to the improvements known as the Agricultural Revolution, the ability of agriculture to provide more food grew.

First census — 1801 — 9 million

1811 — 10 million

Other factors were also conducive to population growth; more infants and children survived to adulthood and more women married younger.

Census every ten years — 1851 — 18 million

1861 — 20 million

After the middle of the eighteenth century, the population began to grow steadily. By the last quarter of the century, the population was growing at an average of 0.9 per cent every year.

1871 — 23 million

1881 — 26 million

1891 — 29 million

By 1811, the population was growing even faster: 1.3 per cent each year.

1901 — 32.5 million

1911 — 36 million

By 1914, it had grown over five times in size.

Population in 1774: 7 million
25% lived in towns

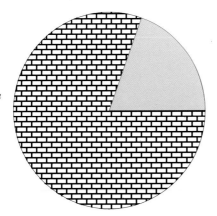

Population in 1911: 36 million
79.9% lived in towns

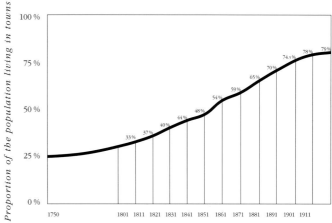

Proportion of the population living in towns

Year

Town: minimum population 2,500–10,000

Source	Year	% of population
Estimate	1750	25%
	1765	
First census	1801	33%
	1811	36.6%
	1821	40%
Regular census every ten years	1831	44.3%
	1841	48.3%
	1851	54%
	1861	59%
	1871	65%
	1881	70%
	1891	74.5%
	1901	78%
	1911	79%

Between 1774 and 1914, the population changed from being predominantly rural to predominantly urban. In 1774 approximately a quarter of the population lived in towns. By 1901, the figure was over three quarters.

In fact, over half the population lived in six huge urban conurbations: London, South East Lancashire, the West Midlands, West Yorkshire, Merseyside and Tyneside.

NUMBER OF HOUSES *(England and Wales)*

    1801   1.6 million

    1911   7.6 million

So 6 million houses had been built

RENT

Generally, rents doubled between 1790 and 1840. After 1840, rents rose more gradually, increasing by a further three quarters by 1910. These increases were mainly due to the larger size and better amenities of the houses themselves.

Ninety per cent of the population rented from private landlords. These landlords included some of the original builders and speculators. However, most of them sold on.

1698	Savery's steam engine
1782	U-Bend Water Seal introduced
1784	Brick tax (*introduced to help pay for wars with France*)
1800	Iron printing presses
1804	Jacquard system of weaving patterns introduced
1807	National Heat & Light Co.
1810	Pall Mall was the first street lit by gas-light Steam-powered printing presses
1824	Self-consuming, plaited candle wicks
1820s	Gas meters becoming available
1830s	Brickmaking by machine
1832	Development of plate glass
1840s	Regular postal service
1844	Mercerised cotton
1847	Mechanical production of tin cans
1850s	Bunsen 'smokeless' gas burners
1852	Synthetic dyes (*aniline dyes made from coal tar; mauve came first*)
1855	Powdered milk
1860	Ten thousand miles of railway track already laid
1860	Horse-drawn trams introduced Paraffin (petrol-based) oil lamps Argand burner
1869	Gas-powered geysers (*economical and convenient way of heating water, especially for baths*)
1869	Margarine
1883	Malted milk
1885	Incandescent gas mantles (*twice as bright and not as sooty*) Two million gas consumers
1890	Electrification of trams Penny-slot gas meters
1897	UK state monopoly of telephones
1900	Twenty thousand miles of railway track already laid
1910	Most new houses have electricity

1774	London Building Act (*other similar local acts followed*)
1820s	Cast-iron pipes begining to replace wooden ones
1835	Municipal Corporations Act
1836	Building Societies Act
1840s	Glazed-stoneware pipes
1844	Metropolitan Building Act
1848	Public Health Act (*created Public Boards of Health which could make local laws*)
1850s	Damp-proof courses introduced
1851	Repeal of Windows Tax Repeal of Glass Tax Repeal of Brick Tax
1858	Local Goverment Act (*more detailed, could make local laws*)
1875	Public Health Act (*much more effective than preceding acts*) Artisans Dwelling Act
1894	Building Act (*later regulations were mainly concerned with light and air. This act relaxed the rules about recessing windows behind a brick reveal*)
1919	Addison Act (*publicly-funded housing for the working classes*)

George III	1760	Coronation of George III	
	1773	American War of Independence begins	*Britain loses her main colony and trading partner*
	1783	Peace with United States of America, France and Spain	
	1793	France declares war on Britain	*Beginning of the French Revolutionary and Napoleonic Wars with France*
	1802	Peace of Amiens	*Short break in wars with France*
	1805	Battle of Trafalgar	*British naval supremacy secured to the benefit of her overseas trade*
	1807	Abolition of slave trade in UK	
George IV & William IV	1811	Regency begins	*George III declared mad – Prince of Wales declared Regent*
	1812	War with United States of America	
	1815	Battle of Waterloo	*End of Revolutionary and Napoeonic Wars*
	1820	Coronation of George IV	*George IV had been Prince Regent since 1811*
	1826	Railways Act	
	1829	Schilibeer's Horsebus	*The original venture was a flop, but buses were here to stay*
	1830	Coronation of William IV	*Younger brother of George IV*
	1832	Great Reform Act Cholera epidemic begins on Tyneside	*Radical shift in political power away from the traditional aristocracy*
	1834	National education begins	
Victoria	1837	Coronation of Queen Victoria	
	1848	Year of Revolutions in Europe	*Only Britain escapes major political upheaval*
		Public Health Act	*Awareness of unhealthy urban conditions provokes a limited response*
	1851	Great Exhibition	*Ten thousand exhibits displayed*
	1854–6	Crimean War	
	1857–9	Indian Mutiny	*Britain threatened with the loss of her major colonial partner*
	1858	The Great Stink	*Ghastly smell of the river Thames empties the House of Commons*
	1860		*550,000 tons of cotton imported from America*
	1861–5	American Civil War	*Cuts off supplies of cotton to Britain's textile towns*
	1864	Embankment scheme, London	*Response to the Great Stink; massive contribution to public health*
	1867	Second Reform Act	*Working–class men get the vote*
	1871	Prince of Wales catches typhus Cheap imports of foreign grain	*Attributed to 'bad plumbing' – heightens public awareness of hygiene* *Further shift in power from the landed classes to the middle classes*
	1875	Public Health Act	*Highly effective legislation on WCs, sewers, water supplies, etc*
	1880	First cargo of frozen meat from Australia	
	1883	Working Men's Trains Act	*Another step towards the development of working-class suburbs*
	1899–1901	Boer War	
Edward VII	1901	Coronation of Edward VII	
	1903	First garden city, Letchworth	*Highly influential on layout of new 'outer' suburbs*
	1910	Coronation of George V	
	1911	Parliament Act	
	1914-18	First World War	*End of the era of speculatively-built housing for rental*

IRONWORK

Late Georgian ironwork was mostly functional and limited in decorative detail. Area railings, balconies and fanlights were made of iron. The railings were usually finished as spear or javelin heads. Elaborate schemes might have been proposed, but the cost often prohibited all but the simplest execution.

From the Regency period, this changed. During the Napoleonic Wars metalwork had greatly improved. After 1815, more ambitious work was possible at less cost. The quality of work was further enhanced by the availability of pattern books and ready-made items.

Larger and more lavishly detailed balconies were supported on newly-developed cantilevered girders. The Indian-inspired verandah provided another opportunity for the stylish use of ironwork.

The conservatory also came into being as a direct result of the advances in ironwork. External staircases, made of cast iron, appeared at the rear of the house.

The profusion of decorative ironwork extended to the interior. Metal staircase railings were used frequently in the larger houses in the second half of the nineteenth century, due to both French influences and the later neo-classical revival.

Entirely new items appeared made of cast iron: a notable example was the toilet-seat bracket. When sanitary fittings replaced the boxed-in patent WCs, the seat was supported by brackets fixed to the wall rather than the bowl.

Another functional item was the coal-hole cover. (Earlier coal-hole covers had been made of stone.) Decorative cast-iron covers date from Queen Victoria's reign.

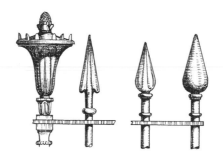

Spear and javelin heads for railings around areas and gardens.

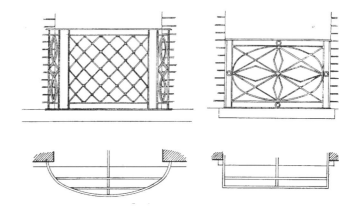

Regency hearts and anthemion designs on a guard rail.

Regency guard rail designs.

Cast-iron balcony with canopy; supported by cantilevers (with details of side elevation shown below right).

Coal-hole covers

Late-Victorian Blenheim pattern for gate and railings.

Late-Victorian arch pattern for gate and railings.

Late-Victorian String Ring pattern for gate and railings.

The sunflower pattern of the Queen Anne Revival.

Queen Anne Revival fanlight design.

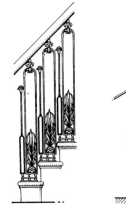

1870s designs for staircase railings showed French influence.

Cantilever brackets for WC seats.

External spiral stairs.

Circular garden seat.

ROOFS

PITCHED ROOFS

The basic roof design was the pitched roof. This was simple to construct and had a functional slope to keep out the weather. The gutter was hidden behind the parapet. The structural timbers were strong enough to take the weight of the covering and its supporting rafters, but had none of the extra tolerance built into modern designs.

A pitched roof which spanned a deep plot had to be very large and, consequently, was highly prominent. Variations in roof design were developed to counter this problem.

VARIATIONS

The mansard could take rooms and be lit by dormer windows. The M-type and the double pitch were less prominent due to their shallower pitches, but were unable to accommodate proper rooms or windows. These types placed the gutters in the 'valley' between the slopes; this could cause problems.

Projecting eaves allowed water to run off, but also had a shallower pitch. They formed an integral part of the rustic Italian look. The use of hips also formed part of this look.

Hipped roofs were a traditonal form that had four slopes instead of two. Hips became most apparent in the suburbs, where pairs of semi-detached houses frequently used hips on their main roofs and tall bays.

The Revivalist forms in the fifty years up to 1914 utilised gables. These required a transverse pitch. Steep roofs were fashionable anyway. The neo-Georgian revival rehabilitated tiles and pantiles as popular alternatives to slate, which had been an almost universal choice of roofing material.

SLATE

Slate, mostly from Wales, became the most common roofing material in the late eighteenth century. Slate is thinly sliced, impermeable stone; it is lighter than brick-based tiles. It had the advantage of allowing the pitch of the roof to be slightly shallower. The traditional alternatives were clay-based tiles or curved pantiles.

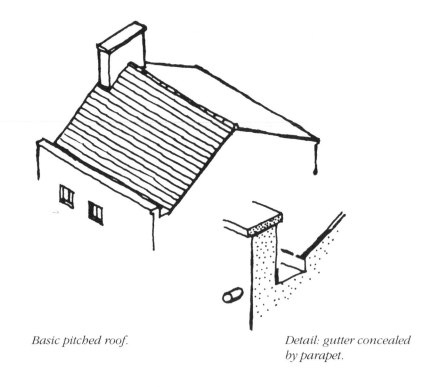

Basic pitched roof.

Detail: gutter concealed by parapet.

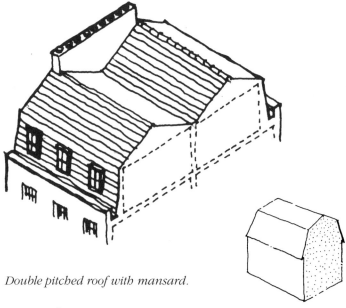

Double pitched roof with mansard.

Detail: mansard.

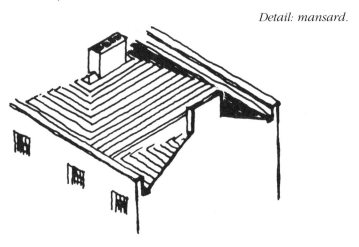

Central valley gutter, also known as M-type or butterfly roof.

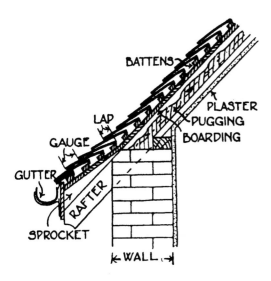

Section of projecting eave.

Rear extension with transverse pitch.

Rustic Italian form, which reintroduced projecting eaves accompanied by supporting brackets.

Half-timbered gable with transverse pitch.

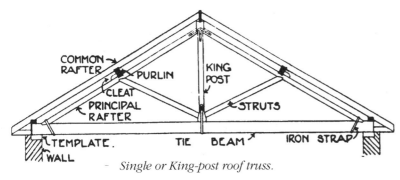

Single or King-post roof truss.

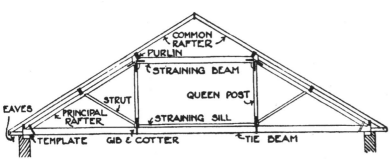

Double or Queen-post roof truss.

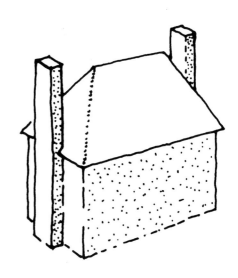

Full circle: steep pitch, hips and tall chimneys were once again fashionable in the years preceding 1914.

171

Staircases were obviously dependent upon the space available. There were three basic designs – the well, the dog-leg and the winder.

The well was the elegant form when space and budget allowed.

The dog-leg was the cheaper alternative, making the maximum use of the space at the end of the hallway.

The winding staircase was crammed into a rear corner of small houses.

Wider plots and larger halls allowed the staircase to be made into something more than merely functional. Screens and arches with fretwork decoration embellished the staircase as halls became reception rooms.

DETAILS

Georgian and Regency staircases had open 'strings' with template scrolls beneath the treads. They were commonly fitted with plain strip balusters and rails.

The hand rail was sometimes the only piece of precious mahogany or oak in the entire house and was proudly left unpainted. Metal balusters were the epitome of elegance, but were mostly confined to grander houses.

Turned and carved balusters were introduced around the middle of the nineteenth century, together with heavy, turned, newel posts. The underside of the staircase was now panelled and cupboards were tucked underneath.

The Queen Anne Revival saw the closed string in favour, sometimes with heavily-moulded detail.

Edwardians boasted some extravagant revivalist staircases with Tudorbethan panelling that could be bought 'off the shelf'.

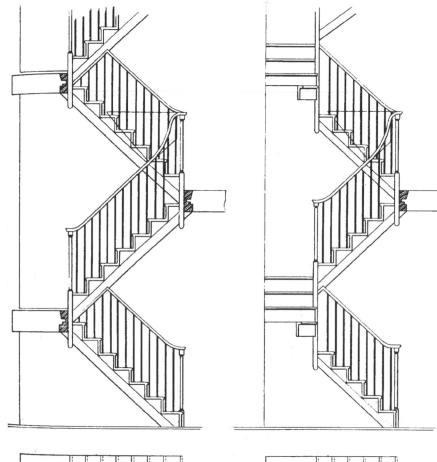

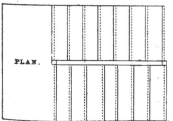

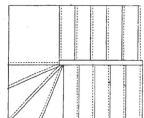

Above left: Dog-leg elevation and plan.

Above right: Winder elevation and plan.

Right: Dog-leg situated at the back of a small house without any rear extension.

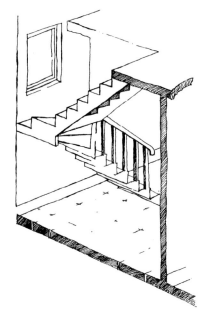

An eighteenth-century joiner's plane.

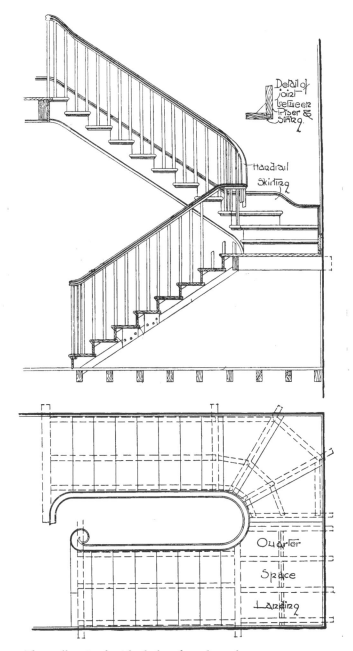

Detail of joint between riser & string.

Handrail

Skirting

The well stair: the ideal plan for a large house.

Quarter

Space

Landing

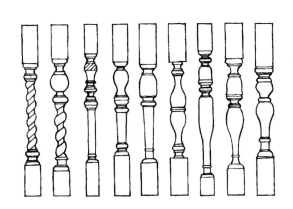

Victorian banister forms.

Mid-Victorian designs of French influence. Ironwork fittings were always up-market.

1870s Tudorbethan design for banister, rail and newel post.

Edwardian revival of panelled, exposed wooden staircase.

MOULDINGS

BASIC SHAPES

The shape of mouldings was ultimately derived from the temple architecture of ancient Greece. These features originally served a purpose, as well as being decorative.

The cornice covered the join between the roof and the wall. It was designed to throw the rainwater off the wall; the fillets acted as drip-moulds. Similar shapes were used on architraves, covering the junction of doors or windows with wall and skirting. They were also used on fireplace surrounds.

Mouldings appeared complex but were actually composed of relatively straightforward elements. These were variations on the flat-faced, right-angled fillet and the curved quadrant.

The quadrant was either concave or convex. The curve could be undercut to emphasise the curve by throwing a shadow. This was called quirking. Curves were used in combination with each other to build up distinctive forms, for example the 'cyma recta'.

The flat fillet served as punctuation to the curved mouldings. It varied in size in proportion to the quadrants, depending on whether it was a supporting or a main element.

Ceiling mouldings were cast from plaster or, later, plaster alternatives. These consisted of central decorations, borders, cornice, coving and possibly a wall frieze below the cornice.

Wood accounted for the rest – architrave, panel decorations, window mouldings, picture, plate and chair rails and skirting.

The predominant shapes of these mouldings changed from one period to another.

CONFUSING NAMES

The shapes were referred to by numerous names. 'Ovolo', which simply meant a convex quadrant, was also known as 'echinus'. (Ovolo is the Latin for 'egg', echinus is the Latin for 'the shell of a chestnut'). 'Cyma reversa' was often, rightly, called 'ogee'. So was cyma recta, which was not appropriate because cyma recta does not follow an ogee curve.

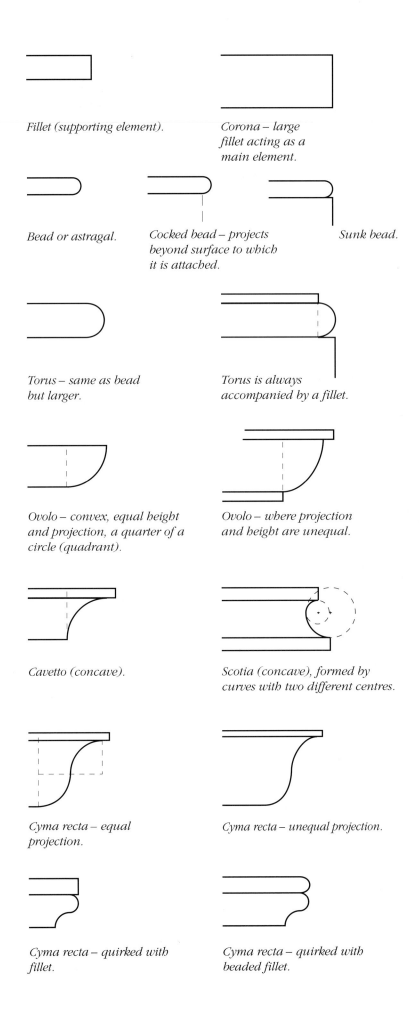

Fillet (supporting element).

Corona – large fillet acting as a main element.

Bead or astragal.

Cocked bead – projects beyond surface to which it is attached.

Sunk bead.

Torus – same as bead but larger.

Torus is always accompanied by a fillet.

Ovolo – convex, equal height and projection, a quarter of a circle (quadrant).

Ovolo – where projection and height are unequal.

Cavetto (concave).

Scotia (concave), formed by curves with two different centres.

Cyma recta – equal projection.

Cyma recta – unequal projection.

Cyma recta – quirked with fillet.

Cyma recta – quirked with beaded fillet.

PERIOD CHARACTERISTICS

Late Georgian handbooks show cyma recta mouldings for architraves, friezes and cornices for doors or windows.

The cyma recta gave a lighter look than its predecessor, the 'bolection'. The bolection had been a characteristic feature of wooden panelling that was replaced by plaster. By the late eighteenth century, plaster covered the main part of the wall from cornice to chair rail, if not the entire wall. The chair rail, above the dado, was a new feature (see WALLS).

In handbooks, the recommended width of an architrave was one sixth of that of the door or opening itself. In practice, this proportion always decreased relative to the size of the house. (This is a good rule of thumb for the whole of the period 1774–1914).

The Regency preference was for a yet lighter look using 'reeded' mouldings. Some variety was created by varying the number of reeds: fewer reeds gave a chunkier look. Alternatively, the shape could be scooped out rather than projecting. This was called 'cavetto'. Reeding was also combined with paterae – square panels, most noticeably used on fireplace surrounds. Doors became fairly plain, with low-relief panels.

The mid-Victorian look was altogether darker and heavier. The most popular moulding was the cyma reversa. Doors now only had four panels, which were often deeper and accommodated mouldings. They were finished in dark paint. The 'torus' design was widely used for skirting boards. The 'frog' hand-rail to the stairs was often the only bit of hardwood in the house and was proudly exposed.

Many more commercial wooden and plaster mouldings became available in the late Victorian period. Both picture/ plate rails and dado returned and the skirting became deeper (see WALLS, COLOUR CHARTS).

Towards the end of the nineteenth century and throughout the Edwardian period, the earlier Georgian preferences for bolection and cyma recta reasserted themselves.

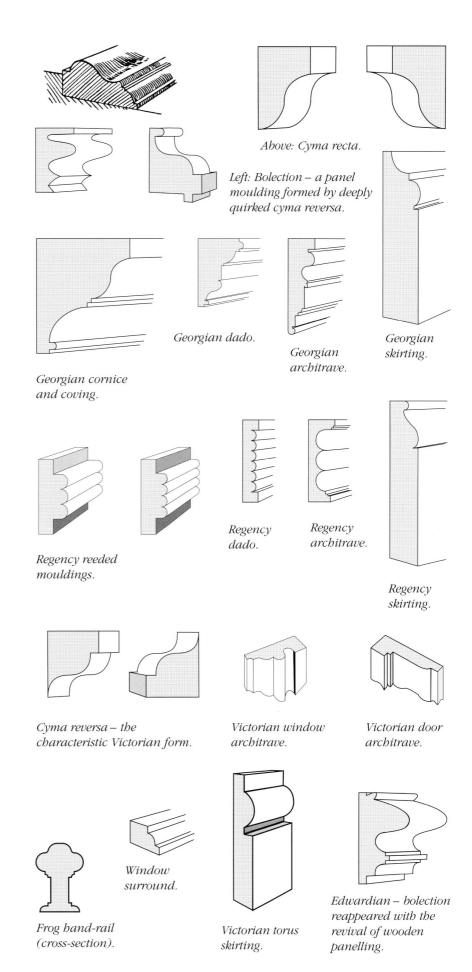

Above: Cyma recta.

Left: Bolection – a panel moulding formed by deeply quirked cyma reversa.

Georgian cornice and coving.

Georgian dado.

Georgian architrave.

Georgian skirting.

Regency reeded mouldings.

Regency dado.

Regency architrave.

Regency skirting.

Cyma reversa – the characteristic Victorian form.

Victorian window architrave.

Victorian door architrave.

Frog hand-rail (cross-section).

Window surround.

Victorian torus skirting.

Edwardian – bolection reappeared with the revival of wooden panelling.

WALLS

SUB-DIVISION

Internal walls were sub-divided for both practical and decorative reasons (see MOULDINGS). It was desirable to cover the junctions between ceiling and wall, window and wall, doorposts and wall and, finally, wall and floor.

Cornice, coving, architrave and skirting could each be given extensive decorative treatment. In the late eighteenth century, the wall itself was either covered in an expensive fabric or wallpaper. More often it was painted with a distemper colour wash. This gave the characteristic pale blue, green, pink or warm grey effects.

CHAIR-RAIL AND DADO

Plastered walls were still a recent development in the 1770s, taking over from wooden panelling at a fraction of the cost. However, they were vulnerable to damage when chairs were placed against them. (When they were not being used, it was the custom to place chairs against the wall in reception rooms.)

To protect plastered walls from being damaged, a 'chair-rail' was fixed three feet up the wall. The area below the rail was known as the dado. The word 'dado' came from the Latin 'die' which meant the base of a classical column.

In the Georgian period, the dado might still be panelled in deal or pine. This was painted a light colour such as 'stone'. Below the dado was the skirting.

Family rooms in large and medium houses of all periods had skirting and architraves. Attic rooms and servants' quarters at the top of the house had skirting but no cornice. Basements of the earlier periods had neither. Later, basement rooms used as parlours would certainly have had skirting. Bedrooms were less likely to have cornices, with perhaps coving instead.

Dining-room tables that stood permanently in the centre of the room were another late eighteenth-century development. Consequently, by the Regency period, chair-rails were disappearing from dining-rooms and also from the library or study.

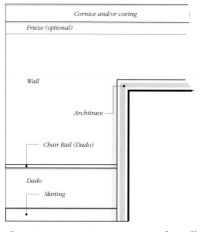

Georgian reception rooms might still have had panelling (wainscot) below the chair-rail.

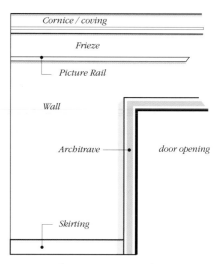

Regency dining-room, study or dressing room.

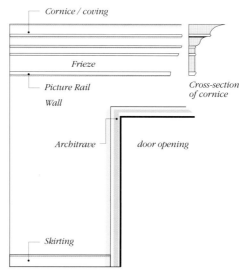

Early Victorian (1850–55) parlour, drawing-room or bedroom.

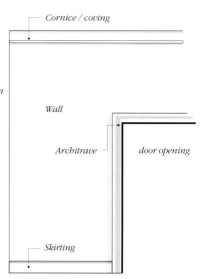

Early Victorian (1850–60) continuous wall from cornice to skirting.

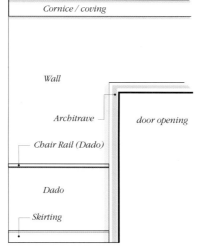

Mid-Victorian parlour (1860–70): return of the dado.

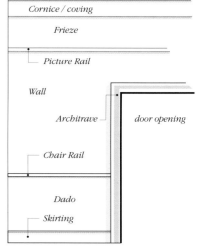

Combination of dado and frieze produced very fussy results.

PICTURE-RAIL AND FRIEZE

Also by the Regency period, the dining-room and library were more likely to have a picture-rail. This addition created an area below the cornice that was the equivalent of the frieze of a classical order. It was usually the more masculine rooms which received this treatment. The more feminine drawing-room generally retained the chair-rail/dado.

The early to mid-Victorian period saw a further series of developments. Up to 1860, the occupants proudly showed off their new machine-made wall-papers on a wall continuous from cornice to skirting. Then the picture-rail and dado made a simultaneous comeback. The results were very fussy. Gradually, those wise enough guided householders towards one or the other; the masculine-feminine character of the rooms once again acting as the arbiter between the choice of frieze/picture-rail or chair-rail/dado. The frieze was deeper than previously. Vertical panels were seen on the walls of stairs and hallways, displaying the brighter, fresher wallpaper designs of the period.

ABUNDANT TILES

The sanitary approach of the late Victorian, Queen Anne Revival period was seen in the abundant use of tiles: right up to the high 'waist' rail in the hall. This was perhaps a foot higher than the chair-rail. The dado below was often papered in an embossed, reinforced paper such as 'lincrusta'.

Bathrooms received similar treatment: everything was hygienically tiled up to the rail. This culminated in the Edwardian bathroom, which had an even higher 'splash' rail and might also have tiles to the top of the wall, including a frieze design.

In the Edwardian hall, the deep frieze was extended outward to form a plate rail. The reintroduction of panelling as part of the Georgian revival brought the story full circle once again. The panelling was painted in light colours, although the original Georgians had never been able to achieve the really white 'whites' of the Edwardians.

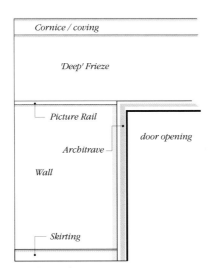

Late-Victorian 'deep' frieze' – the wise decision was either frieze or dado.

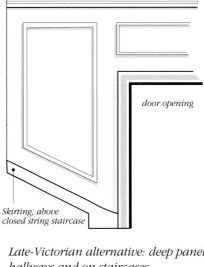

Late-Victorian alternative: deep panels in hallways and on staircases.

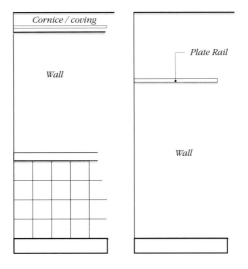

Late-Victorian bathroom, with tiles below the 'splash' rail (left). Kitchen with plate rail and skirting (right).

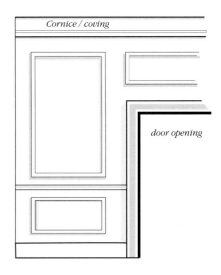

Edwardian return to panelling in halls (large and medium) and drawing-rooms (large only).

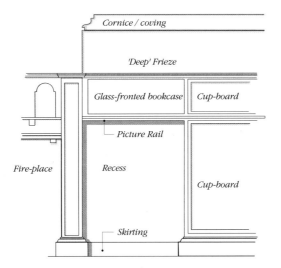

Built-in overmantel, bookcase and cupboards following Georgian forms.

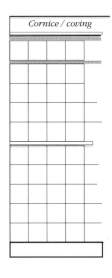

Edwardian bathroom: tiled to the cornice with frieze decoration.

AEDICULA window or door emphasised by means of surround and pediment, so as to appear to be a miniature classical temple. Intended to replace columns as principal decorative features on classically-influenced facades. Widespread from the 1840s onwards.

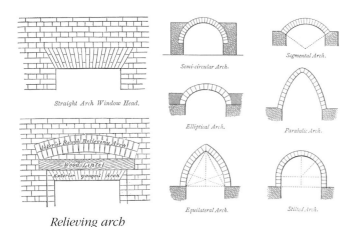

Straight Arch Window Head.

Semi-circular Arch.

Segmental Arch.

Elliptical Arch.

Parabolic Arch.

Equilateral Arch.

Stilted Arch.

Relieving arch

ARCH structural part of wall over an opening; eg, door or window.

AREA open space at basement level in front of a house. Allows basement to be lit by windows. Access was by stone steps, leading down from the street – a recent development in the late eighteenth century.

ARCHITRAVE lowest structural part of entablature, forming a lintel and uprights surrounding an opening (*See* **ENTABLATURE**).

ASHLAR stone hewn so it could be laid square with finely-fitting joints.

ASTYLAR means without columns or pilasters. The astylar terrace was so named because it lacked the giant columns on its facade; astylar terraces became standard after 1840.

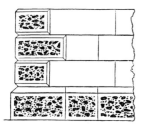
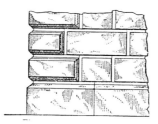

Ashlar stone blocks with cornerstones picked out (quoining) by chamfering the edges and also worm-holing (left).

Designs for Windows

Aediculae

ATTIC room in the roof or upper storey of a building, often half hidden behind the parapet.

BALCONY external walkway accessible from inside the house.

BALCONET shallow projection outside a full-length window or door guarded by a railing.

BALUSTER supporting post of hand-rail, usually decorated (*See* **STAIRS** p.172–73).

BALUSTRADE series of balusters supporting a rail or coping; identifiable as an Italianate feature, common from 1840s onwards.

Cornice and Balustrade.

BARGEBOARD vertically-hung boards which protected the ends of the rooftimbers (eaves) from the weather; vernacular feature, in keeping with Gothic style.

Bargeboards, surmounted by a tall finial.

BATTLE OF STYLES classical versus Gothic, a debate that was fiercely contested in the Regency and mid-Victorian periods, especially over the commissioning of prominent public buildings. Speculative builders preferred to play safe, especially where the Gothic was concerned, for the most part confining themselves to surface decoration.

BAY WINDOW window projecting out from the face of the building on one or more storeys, from the lowest level upwards.

GLOSSARY

BLOCKING COURSE continuation of the wall past the junction of wall and roof to conceal the eaves, also known as a parapet (*See* **BRACKET**, **CORNICE**, **PART-PARAPET**) In the diagram (right), **B** = the blocking course, **C** = cornice, **S** = string course(s). **P** = plinth and **y** = bracket(s).

BRACKET projection designed as a support.

BULL'S EYE round opening or detail (S*ee* **WINDOWS** p.142–43).

BURTON, James (1761–1837) one of the greatest speculators and developers. Without his assistance, Nash's highly influential Regent's scheme would have flopped. James's son, Decimus, became an architect of note.

CAPITAL decorative top of a column immediately below architrave (*See* **ENTABLATURE**).

CASEMENT window (or door) hinged on vertical side

CHIMNEYPIECE decorative surround to fireplace (*See* **FIREPLACES** p.130–1).

CHIMNEYBREAST structural part of a chimney, containing fireplace and flues carrying smoke up from other fireplaces directly below (*See* **CHIMNEYS** p.128–9).

CLASSICAL STYLE style of decoration originating in ancient Greece and Rome, depending on symmetry, proportion and an ordered vocabulary of ornament (*See* **PALLADIAN PROPORTIONS**, **ENTABLATURE**).

CLOSET small, private room often for storage or the intimate conduct of bodily functions.

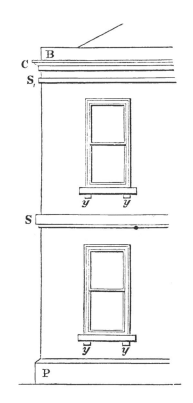

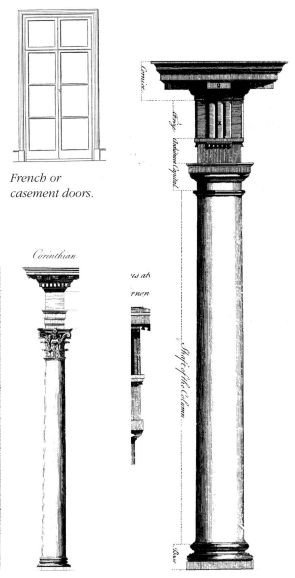

French or casement doors.

GLOSSARY

COADE STONE form of ceramic (fired clay) promoted and mass-produced from 1769 onwards by Eleanor Coade. Used for decorative features both internally and externally. Factory finally closed in 1840.

COPING protective capping or covering to a wall, gable, parapet or balustrade, sloped to carry off water.

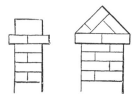

Brick coping

CORNICE upper projecting part of classical entablature; designed to stop rain running down the face of the building (See **ENTABLATURE**).

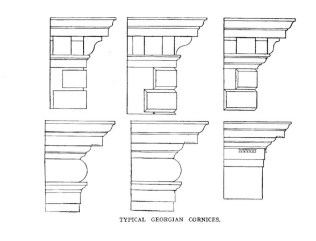

TYPICAL GEORGIAN CORNICES.

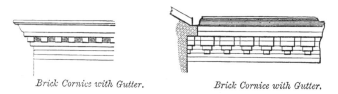

Brick Cornices with Gutter.   *Brick Cornice with Gutter.*

Brick cornices surmounted by cast-iron gutters.

COURSE continuous layer of brick or stone of equal height in a wall. The course surmounting the wall is the blocking course. The wall may be sub-divided by a string course. The plinth completes the wall at the base (See **BLOCKING COURSE, STRING COURSE**).

COVE curved piece, usually joining wall to ceiling (See **MOULDINGS**).

CUBITT, Thomas (1778–1855) perhaps the archetypal speculator, developer, builder and planner. He disdained architects and preferred to refer to himself as a master-builder.

DADO a base, from the Italian word 'die'. Originally, it referred to the base of a column. After the introduction of the chair-rail, it was also applied to the section of an internal wall between the chair-rail and skirting.

DORMER WINDOW window projecting from the slope of a roof and possessing a roof of its own (See **WINDOWS** p.142–3).

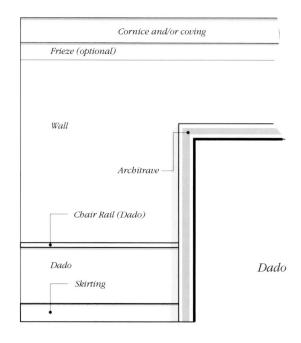

Dado

EAVES structural part of the roof where it meets the wall. The ends were always protected from the weather, either by a parapet or later – when they were allowed to project – by bargeboards, plaster or brackets.

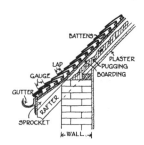

EDWARDIAN King Edward VII succeeded Queen Victoria as monarch in 1901. He himself died in 1910 and was succeeded by King George V. *The Period House: Style, Detail & Decoration* identifies the period as extending from 1900 to 1914 when the First World War began. This period saw a multiplicity of architectural forms, which drew from both classical and vernacular traditions. Architects were, once again, influential – most notably Lutyens, for his reinterpretation of late Georgian forms. The neo-Georgian designs of Lutyens and others were increasingly taken up by the 'spec' builders in the years immediately preceding 1914.

ELEVATION all the parts of a building facing in one direction.

ENCAUSTIC TILE See **TILES** p.162–3.

ENTABLATURE Classical lintel comprising architrave (main structural component), decorative frieze and cornice (See **ARCHITRAVE**, **CORNICE**, **FRIEZE**, **LINTEL**).

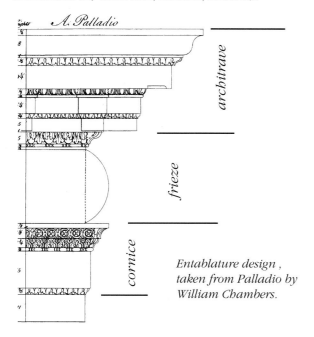

Entablature design, taken from Palladio by William Chambers.

FACADE face of a building, usually the principal one.

FANLIGHT window above the front door, intended to light the hallway, originally semi-circular and often decorated with radiating bars in the shape of a fan (See **WINDOWS** p.142–3).

FINIAL ornament crowning a gable or roof ridge.

FLEMISH BOND See **BRICK** p.146–7.

FRENCH WINDOW Casement door, fully glazed (See **WINDOWS** p.142–3).

Gable

FRIEZE part of a wall between the cornice and picture rail (See **ENTABLATURE**).

GABLE upper part of a wall rising into the roof.

GEORGIAN STYLE *The Period House: Style, Detail & Decoration* illustrates the late Georgian form of urban domestic building of the period 1774–1810. This was the most severe phase of a whole period of development based upon classical, Palladian principles which began in the seventeenth century, well before King George I actually came to the throne (1714) (See **CLASSICAL**, **PALLADIAN**). The period of the Regency is treated separately in this book (See **REGENCY**).

GLAZING BAR support for panes of glass set within the window-frame (See **WINDOWS** p.142–3).

GOTHIC style of architecture developed in the Middle Ages. It depended on pointed arches, ribbed vaults and buttresses for its structure and used a significantly different vocabulary of ornament to classical style. It was revived many times. Eighteenth-century use was largely a substitution of Gothic ornament for classical. During the nineteenth century, proponents such as Pugin argued that Gothic, which had developed in an age of Christian faith, was morally superior to classical architecture, which derived from the pagan temple architecture of Ancient Greece and Rome. The use of Gothic was more public than private. Speculative builders didn't really deviate very far from standard plans, but incorporated features such as vertical emphasis and polychromatic, surface decoration.

Frets, or Guillochis of Various Sorts.

GUILLOCHE ornament in the form of braid.

GUTTER trough usually at base of roof, designed to catch rainwater and channel it to down pipe.

GLOSSARY

HEARTH literally the fire-proof base of a fireplace. Usually made of stone, which had to be supported structurally.

HIP Part of a pitched roof, angled outwards, usually at the corner (*See* **ROOFS** p.170–1).

INGLE, INGLENOOK space under a firehood or beside a fireplace.

ITALIANATE *See* **RENAISSANCE STYLE**.

JERRY BUILDING term used to describe shoddy, inadequate or downright bad work; from the nautical expression 'jury-rig', meaning temporary repairs to masts and rigging. In practice, jerry building usually meant skimping on materials or labour. For example, using up any half-bricks in place of headers, resulting in the inner and outer layers of a brick wall remaining 'unbonded' and therefore structurally weak.

JONES, Inigo (1573-1652) the first English architect to apply the Palladian approach to classical proprtions. Jones was the King's Surveyor. One of his innovations was the first up-market terraced housing in Covent Garden, London.

LANDING space at the top of a staircase.

LATTICE WINDOW window with diamond or square-shaped, leading panes.

LINTEL flat, structural top of an opening (*See* **ARCH**).

LEAN-TO out-building or extension partly supported by the main building.

LOFT low upper room open to the roof.

LOUVRE ventilation opening covered with slats to re-duce entry of both rain and light.

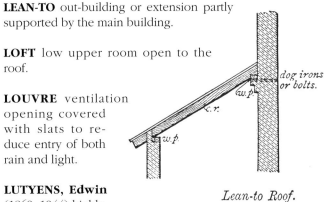

Lean-to Roof.

LUTYENS, Edwin (1869–1944) highly-influential architect who began in the vernacular, Old English style, but became enchanted by what he called 'the high game of classicism'. His work was highly inflential in the neo-classical revival of the Edwardian era.

MEWS originally where hawks were kept, but after the seventeenth century mews meant the row of stables. Ideally, the mews were built at the back of townhouses with accommodation for servants on the first floor, stables and storage for vehicles on the ground floor.

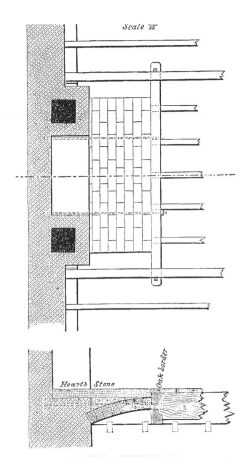

Construction of a hearth: plan and cross-section.

MODILLION projecting bracket, usually supporting cornice (*See* **BRACKET**).

MORRIS, William (1834–96) artist and designer, leading light of the Arts and Crafts movement. His wallpapers were his most notable contribution to popular decor.

MORTAR mixture of sand, lime and sometimes clay, used to bind bricks and stones together.

MULLION vertical framed member of an opening such as a window (*See* **WINDOWS** p.142–3).

MUNTIN *See* **DOORS** p.144–5.

NASH, John (1752–1835) the favourite architect and developer of the Prince Regent. Some of his designs were decades ahead of the times, particularily his use of villas and Italianate forms. His terraces were grander and more imposing than their late-Georgian predecessors.

OLD ENGLISH originally the rural form of the Queen Anne Revival, Old English was characterised by its romantic adoption of vernacular features such as half timbering. It really came into its own as part of the speculative builders' repertoire in the Edwardian period.

ORIEL projecting window bracketed out from wall.

GLOSSARY

PALLADIO, Andrea (1508–80) sixteenth-century Italian who studied and checked the proportions listed by the ancient Roman architect Vitruvius. He published his conclusions, which were in turn checked by Inigo Jones while he was himself in Italy. The Palladian approach to proportion and decoration gained virtually universal sway during the course of the eighteenth century.

PALLADIAN PROPORTIONS *(illustrated opposite)* speculative builders simplified Palladian proportions down to a modular approach, based on **the circle and the square.** (The diameter of the circle was the same as the width of the square.) The width of the window formed the basic module, which was one square/circle wide. The **whole facade** was composed of modules. The most prestigious parts of the house (eg, the first-floor windows) received the most expansive treatment, usually two modules deep for a large house. Although the height was an exact number of modules, the width of an individual house often was not. It was the overall proportions of the terrace that took priority over the individual dwellings.

Another unit used in the classical scheme was the **Golden Rectangle** *(illustrated opposite)*. This took its depth from the diagonal of the square. Its width remained that of the square. This was preferred for ground and second floors of a large house. The proportions were 7:5. The depth of windows on other floors might revert to the square. This was also the width of the 'pier' between the windows of the house.

PANTRY store-room for food, originally flour and bread – later associated with the butler, the senior household servant.

PANTILES brick roofing tiles usually red, curved in section (*See* **TILES** p.162–3).

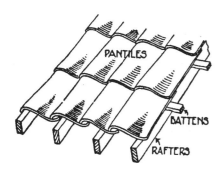

PARAPET top of wall, sometimes projecting above the roof (*See* **BLOCKING COURSE**).

PARGETING plasterwork, usually decorated with inscribed or raised patterns (*See* **BLOCKING COURSE**).

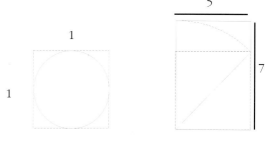

Circle/square: the basic unit　　*The Golden Rectangle*

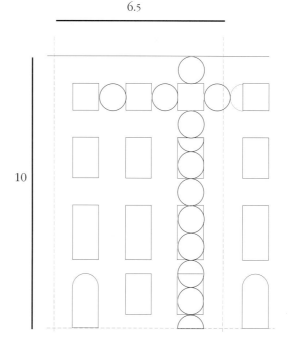

Composition of a facade in units

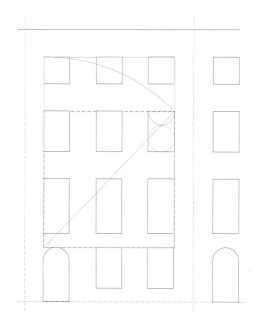

Facade with Golden Rectangle

GLOSSARY

PARLOUR private room, accessible by an internal door – a major aspiration for those who lived in small houses. A room of this kind could be set aside for receiving guests and special occasions. During the nineteenth century, the designation 'parlour' was favoured by the working class and consequently avoided by the middle class. Originally, the parlour was the room in a monastery where guests were received – from the French word 'parler', meaning to speak.

PART-PARAPET half-parapet that protects the underside of the eaves. The gutter itself conceals the edge of the slates or tiles.

PATERA flat, round ornament in classical style, like a rosette (*See* **PATTERNS** p.154–9).

PEDIMENT formalised classical gable, used to emphasise a part of the building.

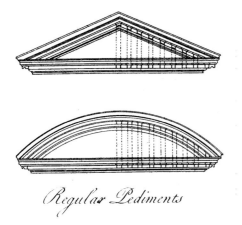

Regular Pediments

PIANO NOBILE Italian term, meaning 'noble storey', that is the most important floor. The piano nobile was situated on the first floor and accommodated the most prestigious room in the house, the drawing-room, where honoured guests were 'received'. The piano nobile gradually fell from fashion during the second half of the nineteenth century as the move out to the suburbs allowed a more expansive ground plan. This was able to accommodate all the reception rooms on the ground floor, with easy access to the garden.

PICTURE RAIL moulding or projection from a wall, situated below frieze. Originally for the hanging of pictures in the hall or library, when it projected far enough to carry an object it became a **PLATE RAIL**.

PILASTER flat projection with the form of a column, used to decorate and articulate a wall or pier.

PITCH angle at which roof slopes upwards from horizontal.

PLATE RAIL *See* **PICTURE RAIL**.

PLINTH projecting base of a wall, column or pilaster (*See* **COURSE**, **BLOCKING COURSE**).

POLYCHROMY literally, decoration in many colours. In practice, the use of coloured brickwork, a characteristic feature of Victorian Gothic; inspired by Italian medieval architecture in the region of Venice, popularised by John Ruskin in his book *The Stones of Venice*.

PORCH projection shielding entrance from the weather.

POST principal vertical structural timber (*See* **ROOFS** p.170–71).

PRIVY small private room, often used for excreting or emptying chamberpots into cesspit. Frequently situated either to the rear or actually outside the house. Also known as the Jericho House or 'jakes'.

PUGIN, Augustus Welby Northmore (1812–52) architect and advocate of the Gothic revival. In his influential book *Contrasts* (1836) he put forward the view that classical architecture was the product of a pagan culture. Consequently, it was not only inappropriate for a Christian country but morally debased. The ideal model for contemporary architecture was that of the Middle Ages, which had developed during an age of Christian faith. Gothic forms, designed by Pugin himself, were adopted for the decoration of the Houses of Parliament. After its completion in 1852, Gothic forms began to appear widely on speculatively-built houses, mainly as decorative features (*See* **GOTHIC**).

QUEEN ANNE REVIVAL style developed by a number of architects that became popular in the 1870s. Loosely based on a mixture of traditional and classical motifs from the reign of Queen Anne (1704–14), the most famous exponent was R. Norman Shaw. The urban form was characterised by red brick and white horizontal banding. It was quickly absorbed into the speculative builders' repertoire, but disappeared around 1900. It was replaced by Old English, which had been introduced as the rural form of the Queen Anne Revival (*See* **VICTORIAN**, **OLD ENGLISH**).

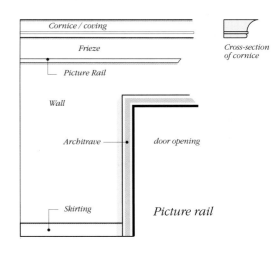

Picture rail

GLOSSARY

QUOIN dressed or rusticated stone or brickwork, which emphasised the corners of a building (See **ASHLAR**).

RAFTER timber on to which roof covering is fixed (See **PANTILES**).

REGENCY the Regency period proper began in 1811 when The Prince of Wales, Prince George, became Regent. He finally succeeded his father to the throne as King George IV. In 1827, he was himself succeeded by his brother, who became King William IV. In *The Period House: Style, Detail & Decoration* we have extended the period covered by the 'Regency' section up to 1850 because medium and small houses did not benefit from the next generation of improvements and stylistic changes until after the middle of the nineteenth century (although Queen Victoria actually came to the throne in 1837). The style was predominantly classical. The period saw the beginnings of villa suburbs but also much unregulated building, which resulted in unhealthy, overcrowded working-class areas of housing.

RENDERING general term for a weatherproof coat on the outside walls of a building.

REVEAL rebate or jamb between the frame of door or window and the outer edge of a wall.

RENAISSANCE STYLE also known as Italianate, Tuscan or Rural Italian. Based on Italian villa architecture of the fifteenth century, its distinctive features were gables with projecting, bracketed eaves, square towers, hipped roofs and pairing of round-headed windows (See **REGENCY**, **VICTORIAN**).

ROCOCO a light, curvaceous form of decoration current during the eighteenth century.

Eighteenth-century rococo decoration

RURAL ITALIAN *See* **RENAISSANCE STYLE**.

RUSKIN, John (1819–1900) fervent advocate of Gothic style, particularly colourful brick Gothic found in the region of Venice, which he popularised through his descriptions and sketches in *The Stones of Venice* (1842).

RUSTICATION deep grooves cut into stone or plasterwork to give the effect of dressed stone (ashlar), mostly used on ground floor (See **ASHLAR**).

SASH WINDOW window whose opening is filled, usually by two vertically-sliding, glazed frames (See **WINDOWS** p.142–3).

SCULLERY small service room, first appeared in the Regency period as plumbing and water supply improved. Washing then began to be separated from cooking, both by location in the scullery and by its inferior status in the hierarchy of chores.

SEMI-DETACHED PLAN pair of houses joined together, usually so that one is the mirror image of the other. Began to appear in great numbers after 1851, as the suburban railway network expanded to cater for increasing numbers of middle-class commuters able to take advantage of

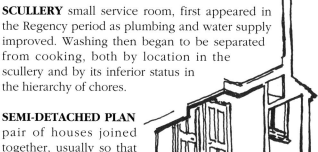

Scullery

cheaper land values further out. Usually broader in width than their terraced equivalents closer to the centre, they no longer needed to locate the services in the basement.

SERVICE ROOM room used to store goods, usually food, and prepare it for cooking.

SHAW, R. Norman (1831–1912) the best known architect of the Queen Anne Revival. His designs for the suburb of Bedford Park, published in *The Builder*, featured both the red-brick, Queen Anne form and the half-timbered Old English form (See **OLD ENGLISH**, **QUEEN ANNE REVIVAL**).

SHUTTERS moveable panels, usually fitted to block windows.

SILL base of wall or window.

SLATE specific type of impermeable stone, which can be split into thin layers – usually for covering roofs or making damp-proof course (See **ROOFS** p.170–71).

SKIRTING panelling at the foot of the wall covering the join with the floor.

GLOSSARY

STOREY floor, particularly the space between the two floors.

Storey floor

STRING timber support for stair.

STRING COURSE single layer of bricks projecting from wall, often at first floor-level in Georgian architecture (See **BLOCKING COURSE, COURSE**).

STUCCO form of patent, hard plaster.

STYLE vertical timber, as in wall or door (See **DOORS** p.144–5).

SWAG also known as festoons, decorative device in a light classical vein.

TERRACE row of joined houses, often similar and designed as a whole but sometimes the work of numerous different builders. Whether or not this showed was due to the degree of control, or lack of it, exercised by the landlord or developer.

TERRACOTTA moulded brickwork, readily available in the last quarter of the nineteenth century.

TILE flat baked clay or split stone slab used for floor, roof or wall covering (See **TILES** p.162–3).

TRANSOM horizontal bar set across an opening such as a window (See **WINDOWS** p.142–3).

TRUSS transverse structural timber designed to support a roof (See **ROOFS** p.170–1).

UPSTAND the continuation of the party wall through the roof by at least one foot to ensure a thoroughly effective firebreak, obligatory by regulations in some areas, including London since 1774.

VERANDAH balcony with roof or awning introduced during the Regency period. Part of a move towards exotica, made possible by advances in metalwork that allowed cantilever girders to become sufficiently cheap and available.

VERNACULAR ARCHITECTURE forms of domestic building indigenous to England and Wales in particular, either developed or traditionally used here; for example, timber-framed, jetty construction.

VICTORIAN Queen Victoria came to the throne in 1837 and reigned until 1901, a period spanning three generations. It was not until mid-century that changes which represented a comprehensive Victorian style affected all three classes – upper, middle and the recently named 'working' class. *The Period House: Style, Detail & Decoration* takes the middle generation, approximately 1850-75, as the basis for its Mid-Victorian section. Further development of Victorian style during the third generation of Victorians is covered in the Late Victorian section. *See* **QUEEN ANNE REVIVAL**. The mid-Victorian style, established in the years 1850-75, was the first heterogenous style – having numerous different forms that shared common elements. These common elements enable it to be identified as a style. The most notable example was the straight-sided, or cant, bay window

VOYSEY, Charles (1857–1941) architect and designer, influenced by Norman Shaw, responsible for popularity of rough-cast finishes, deep gables and numerous other vernacular features picked up by speculative builders in Edwardian suburbs. His work embodied the motto 'Fitness is the basis for beauty'.

FURTHER INFORMATION

Name	Address & Tel No	Additional info

DECOR

Dulux
ICI Paints, Wexham Road, Slough, Berks SL2 5DS
Telephone: 01753 550555

Heritage collection of authentic paint colours, containing Georgian, Victorian and Edwardian ranges

Baer & Ingram
152 Walton Street, London SW3 2JJ
Telephone: (0181) 581 9077

Reproductions of Georgian wallpapers

Hamilton Weston
18 St Mary's Grove, Richmond, Surrey TW9 1UY
Telephone: (0181) 940 4850

Modern reproductions of historic wallpapers, archive and reference library

Paper and Paints Ltd.
4 Park Walk, London SW10 0AD
Telephone: (0171) 352 8626

Paint and colour specialists who produce ranges ranges of paintbased on colours used by eighteenth and nineteenth-century house-painters

Temple Newsam House
Temple Newsam House, Leeds LS15 0AE
Telephone: (01532) 647321

Wallpaper archive, restoration advice and public exhibitions

The Wallpaper Society
Can be contacted through the Victoria & Albert Museum

Zoffany
63 South Audley Street, London W1Y 4BF
Telephone: (0171) 629 9262

Zoffany reproduce a collection of historic wallpapers found at Temple Newsam House

Colefax & Fowler
39 Brook Street, London W1

MUSEUMS & COLLECTIONS

Victoria & Albert Museum
Cromwell Road, London SW7 2RL
Telephone: (0171) 938 8500

Department of Furniture Interiors

Jeffrye Museum
Kingsland Road, London E2L
Telephone: (0171) 739 9893

Period room sets

NATIONAL BODIES

National Trust
36 Queen Anne's Gate, London SW1H 9AS
Telephone: (0171) 222 9251

Department of the National Heritage
Heritage Division, 2-4 Cockspur Street,
London SW1Y 5DH
Telephone: (0171) 211 6372 *General Enquiries*

Listed buildings, conservation, etc

FURTHER INFORMATION

NATIONAL BODIES *(continued)*

English Heritage
Fortress House, 23 Savile Row, London W1X 1AB
Telephone: (0171) 973 3000

Conservation and restoration advice

Architectural Heritage Fund
27 John Adam Street, London WC2N 6HX
Telephone: (0171) 925 0199

Society for the Preservation of Ancient Buildings
37 Spital Square, London E1 6DY
Telephone: (0171) 377 1644

PERIODICALS & PLACES TO VISIT

Period Living and Traditional Homes magazine
EMAP Elan, Victory House, 14 Leicester Place,
London WC@H 7HP
Telephone: (0171) 437 9011

Monthly magazine aimed at 'all those romantic souls … living in a period home'. Each issue contains a classified directory of products & services as well as features

18 Folgate Street
18 Folgate Street, London E16 BX
Telephone: (0171) 247 4013

Visit this early Georgian house where each room has been set as if its original occupants have just left it

INFORMATION & ADVICE

Architectural Antique Search
Cliffe Cottages, Parsons Green, Wetherby,
West Yorks LS22 4RF

Will buy or locate architectural salvage piece required by client

Garden History Society
Station House, Church Lane, Wickwap,
Wooton-under-the-Edge, Gloucs GL12 8NB
Telephone: (01455) 294888

Georgian Group
37 Spital Square, London E1 6DY
Telephone: (0171) 377 1722

Conservation group, providing information, visits and events

Victorian Society
1 Priory Park Gardens, Bedford Park,
London W4 1TT
Telephone: (0181) 994 1019

Information and events for the Victorian period

British Decorators Association
6 Haywra Street, Harrogate,
North Yorkshire HG1 5BL

Over 1,000 members who specialise in the decoration of period homes

The Brooking Collection
Woodhay, White Lane, Guildford,
Surrey GU4 8PU

Unique record of the development of period detail. Information and advice available

BIBLIOGRAPHY

Adams S	The Arts and Crafts movement			
Architectural Review	Recent Domestic Architecture	Architectural Review		1908
ed. Artley A	Putting Back the Style		Evans Bros	1982
Aston M & Bond J	Landscape of Towns	London	Dent	1976
Barrett H & Phillips J	Suburban Style (1840-1960)	London	Macdonald Orbis	1987
Blackburne E	Suburban and Rural Architecture			1865
Bosomworth D	Victorian Catalogue of Househod Goods	London	Studio Editions	1992
Boxer M	Liverpool			
Brunskill R W	Illustrated Handbook of Vernacular Architecture			
Byrne A	London's Georgian Houses	London	Georgian Press	1986
Caffyn L	Workers' Housing in West Yorkshire	London	HMSO	1986
Calder J	Life in the Victorian Home	Blandford	Batsford	1979
Cave C F	The Smaller English House			
Chambers W	Treatise on Decorative…Architecture	London		1791
Chapman S D	History of Working-Class Housing			
Cranfield & Potter	Houses for the Working Classes			1904
Cruickshank D & Burton N	Life in The Georgian City	London	Viking	1990
Cruickshank D & Wyld P	London: the Art of Georgian Building	London	Architectural Press	1975
Curtis A	Small Garden Beautiful	London		1909
Dillistone G	Planning & Planting of Little Gardens	London		1920
Day L F	Ornamental Design			1897
Doré G	London: A Pilgrimage	(reproduction: Dover Press)		1871
Dyos H J	A Victorian Suburb	Leicester	University Press	1961
Eberlein H D & Richardson A	Smaller English House	London	Batsford	1925
Fletcher B	The English House	London		1910
Foley E	Book of Decorative Furniture	London		1920
Gardiner S	Evolution of the House			
Gibberd F	Architecture of England	London		1791
Girouard M	Cities and People			

BIBLIOGRAPHY

Girouard M	Sweetness and Light			
Gray R	History of London	London	Hutchinson	1984
Hadfield M	History of British Gardening	Edinburgh	John Murray	1979
Hamilton J	An Introduction to Wallpaper	London	HMSO	1983
Helm W	Homes of the Past	London	Bodley Head	1921
Hobhouse H	Thomas Cubitt: Master-builder			
Holme C	Modern British Domestic Architecture	London	The Studio	1901
Huggett F E	Victorian England as seen by *Punch*			
Jackson N	Speculative Housing in London	Ph.D thesis (Univ. Westminster)		1990
Jenner M	Architectural Heritage of Britain and Ireland	London	Penguin	1992
Johnson A	How to Restore your Victorian House	Devon	David & Charles	1991
Kaufman M	Housing of the Working Classes			1975
Kerr R	The Gentleman's House			1865
Langley B	The Builder's Jewel			1767
Lichten F	Decorative Art of Victoria's Era	London		1950
Long H	The Edwardian House	Manchester	University Press	1993
Loudon J C	Cottage, Form and Villa Architecture			1846
Macintosh C	Book of the Garden	Edinburgh		1853
Marshall J & Wilcox H	The Victorian Home			
Mayhew T	London Labour and the London Poor			
Middleton G	Modern Buildings Vol 2	London	Caxton	c. 1910
Morris T	A House for the Suburb			1870
Moss P	Town Life Through the Ages			
Muthesius H	The English House			1903
Muthesius S	The English Terraced House	Yale	University Press	1982.
Nicholson P	Builder's and Workman's New Directory	London	Knight & Lacey	1825
Olsen D J	City as a Work of Art: London, Paris and Vienna	Yale	University Press	1986
Osband L	Victorian House Style	Devon	David & Charles	1991
Pain W	Builder's Companion	London		1762

BIBLIOGRAPHY

Palmer R	History of the Water-Closet			
Parissien S	Regency Style	London	Phaidon	1992
Pugin A W N	Contrasts			1836
Quennell C H B	Modern Suburban Houses			1906
Quennell P & D	History of England Vols III & IV			
Quiney A	House and Home			
Quiney A	Period Houses	London	George Philip	1989
Reyburn W	Flushed with Pride: The Story of Thomas Crapper		London/Pavilion	1989
Richardson C J	Picturesque Designs for Mansions	London	Atchley	1870
Rivington's series on	Building Construction	London	Longman's	1893
Robinson W	English Flower Garden	London	John Murray	1899
Stamp G & Goulancourt A	The English House 1860-1914	London	Faber & Faber	1986
Stevenson J J	House Architecture			1880
Summerson J	Georgian London			
Unwin R	Cottage Plans and Common Sense			1902
Waller P J	Town, City and Nation: England 1850-1914	Oxford	University Press	1983
Walvin J	English Urban Life 1776-1851	London	Hutchinson	1984
Wheeler G	A Choice of Dwelling	London	John Murray	1871
Williams T	History of Invention		Macdonald Orbis	
Woodforde J	Georgian Houses for All			
Yarwood D	The English House		Batsford	1979
Young & Marten	Victorian House Catalogue	London	Sidgwick & Jackson	1990
Young W	Town and Country Mansions and Suburban Houses			1879
Surveys	City of London Survey Vols XXI, XXV, XXVI, XXXIII, XXXVI, XXXIX, XLII		London	
Periodicals	The Builder, Building News, Building World, The Graphic, The Illustrated London News			

© 1996 Richard Russell Lawrence and Teresa Chris

First published in 1996 by
George Weidenfeld & Nicolson Limited
The Orion Publishing Group
Orion House
5 Upper St. Martin's Lane
London WC2H 9EA

British Library Cataloguing-in-Publication Data
A catalogue record for this book is available
from the British Library.

ISBN 0 297 83294 8

Designed by Richard Russell Lawrence.

Water-colour illustrations on the opening pages by
Richard Russell Lawrence.

Printed and bound in Great Britain by
Butler & Tanner Ltd, Frome and London.